THE ETHICS OF COMPROMISE

and the art of containment

T. V. Smith, formerly professor of philosophy at the University of Chicago, is now Maxwell Professor of Citizenship and Philosophy at Syracuse University. Long editor of the *International Journal of Ethics,* he continues to serve on its editorial board (now *Ethics*). He has been a member both of the Illinois Senate and of the U.S. Congress. During World War II he was director of education for the Allied Control Commission in Italy, a member of the MacArthur educational mission to Japan, and a member of the first U.S. educational mission to Germany.

Professor Smith is the author of a number of books, including *The Philosophic Way of Life, Beyond Conscience, The Democratic Tradition in America, Atomic Power and Moral Faith,* and *Man's Threefold Will to Freedom.* He is also the co-author of such books as *Foundations of Democracy* (with Robert A. Taft), *A Study of Power* (with C. E. Merriam and H. D. Lasswell), and *The Democratic Way of Life* (with Eduard C. Lindeman). In 1951 the Beacon Press published his *Abraham Lincoln and the Spiritual Life.*

The Ethics of Compromise

AND THE ART OF CONTAINMENT

T. V. SMITH

STARR KING PRESS • BOSTON

TO OLD MINDS

AND YOUNG HEARTS

Contents

THE ETHICS OF COMPROMISE

and the art of containment

1. The Logic of Presumption

I. *Orientation*

If language were as simple as sectarians are simple-minded, there would be no use for unabridged dictionaries. Infants are born to babble, but men are destined to endeavor to communicate. Communication need not create community—not above the level of imprecation—but lack of communication is certain to disrupt or frustrate community. Verbal symbols are furnished us free; they are indeed indispensable in the growth of personality, but they are cantankerous contrivances—vague when we need them precise, and at the best ambiguous when we need them univocal. "If truth were self-evident," says Cicero, "eloquence would not be necessary." Nor would semantics have become the concern it is today.

So unquiet is the resulting human situation that the best we can hope for, as touching the most precious value symbols in use among us, is but a sad success in the struggle for clarity, a frustrating endeavor in the high art of communication. One does not have to go to Moscow for illustration; he need go only to Evanston—or, sadder still, to Rome.

3

Leaving concrete cases to await their turn, we recommend for a modest start the caution of Aristotle that it is "the mark of an educated man to look for precision in each class of things just so far as the nature of the subject matter admits; it is evidently equally foolish to accept probable reasoning from a mathematician and to demand from a rhetorician [politician] scientific proof."

So vast, however, is the sea of dissidence upon which we now embark in the name of community that we do well to reduce the responsibility of the present essay. We begin with the question of ambiguity, but we shall not end short of the whole problem of compromise. Language lacks are not our theme, but the cultural or even cosmic dubiety which linguistic ambiguity often reflects. To compromise or to contain—that would seem to be the only option short of suicide. So it is not our thought that important problems can be solved by manipulating symbols, but ambiguity can show us where the problems are. The best semantics cannot solve the worst of our problems, but bad semantics can prevent the solution of any and all problems.

Having said so much, let us observe now a moral aspect of semantics, an aspect all too little regarded in an age of logic. It is this aspect which concerns us chiefly—chiefly but not exclusively—for the ethical problem arises from a perverse approach to the logical. The simplest form of verbal vagueness is ambiguity. The way men treat ambiguity can become, and indeed does chronically become, a moral problem. Assuming that language exists not to confuse but to clarify, not to balk but to facilitate communication, we are nevertheless face to face with the fact that ambiguity confuses meaning, may frustrate communication, and at times can tax to the breaking point the forbearance of men engaged in a common enterprise.

Yet ambiguity is, as the philosophers like to say, a "given"—that is, a radical and observable fact, visible in many an effort to communicate. Others, that is to say, may be as intelligent as we are, may understand us clearly enough, and still be in disagreement with us about the most serious convictions. To clarify further, other men may be as honest as we are, may clearly understand us, and still be in disagreement with us about the most sacred concerns of life. Disagreement, no less than agreement, may be communicated through symbolism. The outcome, whatever the intent, of communication is oftentimes disagreement. Indeed, dissidence may be the test as well as the result of communication. To pre-judge the issue of ambiguity is itself the most fatal prejudice indulged in by human beings. It is the source indeed of the most unmagnanimous conduct. It is the fountainhead of fanaticism.

However we assess the observable fact of dissidence, its presence, its "givenness" is enough to foredoom political conventions to "strategic obfuscation," ecumenical conferences to futility, and learned congresses to sterile abstractions— enough to subject the common life to fear, if not to the perpetrations of fanaticism. Let me make even more concrete what it is that I mean.

I once had a letter from a beloved old friend of my youth in Texas, a wise though barely literate ranchman. He wrote substantially this: "Now that you are 'eddicated' in a northern university and are teaching philosophy, please to tell me simply where I can find the real meaning of words." I could reconstruct from memories of arguments overheard in childhood the type of predicament which led him to this simple and pathetic question.

He had, little doubt, been frustrated in communication by arguing with some neighbor about matters of deep concern to both: about baptism, very likely, for it was a sectarian community deep in the "Bible Belt." Now whether a man were baptized would be to both disputants a matter of eternal life—or of everlasting death. One had been "sprinkled," let us guess; the other had been "immersed." Somebody had, then, not been "baptized." Appeal was made to the dictionary, where both meanings were most probably given—one, two. This was ambiguity with far too much at stake to be let alone. Appeal would then be made, through men more learned, to a Greek lexicon. But this honest effort to get closer to the source of inspired meaning was probably rewarded with the same devilish ambiguity, this time quite probably in "two, one" order.

Where, then, does one find the real meaning of terms? To me his appeal was most embarrassing. To write my old friend what I supposed to be the truth—that each meaning was equally "real"—would be, from his point of view, to trifle with his affections, indeed would be to treat trivially his eternal destiny.

Nor is this type of perturbation confined to simple men, face to face with dissidence over sacred symbols. I have known an international congress of philosophers to meet the same problem so frustratingly as to provoke a major philosopher (it was F. C. S. Schiller at Prague in 1934) to propose an interruption of the substantial business of seeking truth and pursuing it, in order to engage in an adjectival interregnum: a commission, as he proposed, to fix the meaning of the basic terms that were being used, so that philosophers might guess from what was being said what was being talked about.

Closer to home in both space and time, I have known a learned conference to confine its agenda two years in succession to the subject of symbols, and in the end to beg the unity which it could not find. I have known, more concretely speaking, an American state legislature to resort to statute in order to resolve the ambiguity of a disputed term. Does "natural law," for instance, mean nature controlling herself as to human reproduction, or nature indulging her full fecundity, whatever quality may emerge from quantity reproduction?

Even the saints quail at these crossroads, as we shall presently see when we turn to the theologians for guidance through or around the semantic jungle. The treatment of ambiguity may indeed become, has in fact already become, a moral matter. For the attitude one takes toward it may lead him to magnanimity: recognition, that is, of equal legitimacy of the point of view of his opponent; or it may also lead him to meanness: denial, that is, that an opponent has a point of view, at any rate a legitimate one. For one to claim innocence in a semantic quandary, where two are *particeps criminis* in ambiguity, is to forfeit all rights of innocence. I will put it even stronger. It is not only odious; it is also impious. Who made me God to insist thus upon being judge of you in my own case?

Let us, for dramatic presentation, think of humanity gathered in a great mass meeting to deal with this problem of ambiguity, to undo the penalty of Babel. In this age, the scientists would demand the first chance to lead the meeting. The theologians would perhaps come next, in this period of reappearing evangelism. They are indeed wholesale merchants of vagueness. Then the philosophers would no doubt insist upon being heard, for they think of themselves (however the world may think) as the overlords of wisdom. All the while, however, there would be lurking on the fringe of our gathering a fourth class, albeit strategically unlisted as participant—the genus *politicus*.

All three of the listed leaders might be glad in the end, I predict, to appeal to this fourth, this unenrolled type, the politician, in order to prevent the three-ringed enterprise from breaking up in a semantic row. The drive for full fraternity among even the best-intentioned men is seldom contained short of fanaticism, unless it be stayed, short of that ugly goal, through political accommodation.

Of the three classes, the scientists find ambiguity the hardest to bear. Confronted with it as a fact, the scientists renounce it as a value. Further, they denounce, on the day shift at least, the fuzzy-edged symbols of common sense, preferring to invent other symbols which can be clearly defined and which remain fixed in meaning—that is, to cut the Gordian knot, heedless of the wasted cord. We non-scientists may envy the resulting vantage in clarity which this gives to the scientists, until we discover that we desperately need for household exigencies the strings which the scientists so audaciously throw away. To change the figure, the scientists throw many a baby (of value) out with the bath water (of unclear symbols).

Now do not misunderstand me. These scientists are fine fellows to have around, when they mind their own business. But, as Emily Dickinson deftly warns:

> Surgeons must be very careful
> When they take the knife!
> Underneath their fine incisions
> Stirs the culprit—Life!

At the very best, scientists can be most annoying in their frequent insistence upon clarity when the generalized needs of life are larger than their specialized concern. Thus to damn ambiguity as a vice to be excised invests scientific purpose with a provincialism all its own. Fine fellows that they are, scientists are the high priests of a single aim, whereas theologians and philosophers are servants of values which include but also transcend the bright light of clarity. We all need clarity at times; and when we need it, we need it badly. But it is not the only need of mankind, and perhaps it is not the most important. Man lives not by logic alone. Ambiguity is the threshold to more value than is clarity, though the

growth which ambiguity prompts finds in clarity
an honorable goal.

No doubt we could describe love in behavioral
terms, à la Kinsey report; but what lover would
be content to leave love there? We could trans-
late the Lord's prayer into the marketplace symbols of give-and-take, or Lincoln's Gettysburg
Address into the poverty of basic English. But
what worshiper would suffer the one, what
patriot would endure the other? Ambiguity can
be banished in the scientific way along narrow
sectors, but at a price too dear. As the scientists
cannot talk any more clearly than we about
many of the things which concern the rest of us,
they may honorably refuse to talk at all. Their
silence we can respect; but if they mutter about
it, they but "murder to dissect." We may pass it
as but a breach of etiquette when they sit on
the sidelines smiling like Cheshire cats; or we
may even regard it as only a matter of aesthetics
when they frown like Sphinxes upon our mud-
dling endeavors, neck-deep in the vague. But it
becomes a moral matter—and here we rise like
men to defend our rights—when the scientists
break their superciliousness to cry, as is their
wont—to cry "nonsense" upon our equally indispensable, if vague, kind of sense. They cannot treat our ambiguity as a vice without themselves becoming tinged with the vicious through
maladroit association.

There is room for both types of leaders—indeed for all three, and for many more besides—if only we can jointly develop the magnanimity toward diverse meanings which the division of ideal labor implies and requires. The scientists clearly think that the rest of us do not know what we are talking about, and it may be merely because what we are talking about is larger than can be contained in their bloodless categories. Let them, then, mind their own business, while we mind ours, that all business high and low may be properly minded. The only honest accounting of the unclear is honorable use of ambiguous symbols. The scientists honorably apart (for they have earned the right to stand apart), we shall continue to converse with one another as best we can of values that are dear through symbols that are hazy.

That is, we shall do this unless the theologians violate their sacred trust and throw us back to darker ages by reversion to semantic provincialism. The scientists may be narrow in a good cause, the indispensable cause of clarity; the theologians may become narrow in a bad cause, the dispensable cause of ideological conformity. They have their own devil to tempt them to treat ambiguity not as a virtue of language, promissory of growth, but as a vice of men, deserving of censure.

Hard indeed to assimilate to any genuinely

cooperative enterprise are men who succumb to the temptation to proclaim the good news of our damnation without first having acquired our consent. "The one thing more difficult than following a régime," says Marcel Proust, "is keeping from imposing it on others." Orthodoxy is a harsh exaction where inevitable ambiguity of language makes us all heterodox in turn. But we shall not damn even these damners of dissidence without giving them a hearing, and we shall make distinction among them wherever they acknowledge the difference in theology between what is generous and what is mean. Meanness does not prove less but more mean by being elevated to the skies and made an attribute of deity.

ii. A Mohammedan Case

We are tempted to hope that our Christian civilization will henceforth prove immune to the temptation thus to transvaluate values by changing their locus. In this generous predisposition, let us first consider what happened, long ago and far away, outside our Judeo-Christian climate of opinion. As our opening illustration of the villainous logic of presumption, let us take a case from the history of Mohammedanism.

Maimonides gives us the example which we need, to make our thought concrete. He tells the story, in connection with the conquest of

Spain, of a certain Moslem conqueror—Ibn Tumart by name—who came to the gates of the Spanish city of Cordova, where resided the ancestors of Spinoza. He called together the Jewish elders and gave them the harsh option common enough in the history of theology, the option of conversion or liquidation. The case is so typical of the theological method of dealing with ambiguity that it will bear direct quotation from Maimonides.

"It is because I have compassion," Ibn Tumart blandly begins with the elders, "that I command you to become Moslem; for I desire to save you from eternal punishment."

The Jews replied: "Our salvation depends on our observance of the Divine Law; you are the master of our bodies and of our property, but our souls will be judged by the King who gave them to us, and to whom they will return; whatever be our future fate, you, O King, will not be held responsible."

But this is but what *they* thought, not at all what *he* thought. They should have known better, for they had historically, as the "chosen people," used the same or similar logic on others. "I do not desire to argue with you, for I know you will argue according to your own religion. It is my absolute will that you either adopt my religion or be put to death."

That they did not do; so *this* he did to them.

There we have the logic of presumption in all its wry and sad immorality. For let us not mince any words as we approach now the crux of our semantic thesis. It is immoral, always and everywhere immoral, for anybody to treat symbols that are ambiguous—such as the will of God in this case—as though they were unequivocal. This is not only immoral; it would appear to be the final form of immorality, the very sin against the Holy Spirit of rationality. Yet the roots of this logic are sunk deep in sacerdotal soil, and its inevitable fruits are an offence to all high-mindedness.

This logic of presumption denies to others, that is to say, *the right it claims for itself, the right to resolve the ambiguous, ex parte.* Look you now how grossly immoral this is. It goes against the Golden Rule in Christian ethics, which calls for an imaginative exchange of roles when confronted with ambiguous claims. It goes against the Kantian "categorical imperative"—that the principle of action, and judgment, should be disinterestedly generalized to include all on equal terms. It goes against the utilitarian principle of felicity, which provides in all application of social norms that "each should count for one and nobody for more than one." This logic is, to summarize, radically immoral, by whatever civilized test we seek to try it. In the light of this age-old

theological offence against ethics, it does not
take a cynic to insist that an honest god *would* be
the noblest work of man.

No sectarianism can get so thick-skinned as not
to exude some guilt over the practice of such
radical immorality. Note the standard way,
then, in which we all work ourselves up to the
alienation from humanity required by such logic.
Let us put it in the first person, since we have
all felt the temptation to surrender to the undertow of such primitive logic. We must manage
somehow to hide from ourselves, lest we be
overcome with guilt, how immoral we can become in the name of religion. We naturally
assume—and the more sacred the symbols, the
easier we appear to assume it—that *our* use of
the given ambiguity is the *only* proper use. Upon
this assumption, we get into an argument, as
unexpectedly as unintentionally, with another,
who makes the same ex parte assumption as we
—namely, that *he* owns the symbol and can
define it as he will.

It quickly becomes manifest that we do not
mean the same thing by the symbols which we
seem to share, but which each insists upon
monopolizing. Where clarity is thus falsely pre-
sumed, only enmity can result. At such moral
crossroads, we then patiently explain what it is
we mean, and are surprised that the other person does not agree with us—*i.e.*, does not "under-

stand us." (He, at the same time, is going through the same frustrating experience with us.) So we undertake kindly to explain ourselves more carefully. In fortunate cases, through these gestures of rational good will—*theological* examples are not, alas, always among the "fortunate cases" —we reach an agreement. That is, we win over our opponent; or he—*mirabile dictu!*—wins us over. We are still speaking of theological cases in which conversion is normally the only satisfactory outcome, but an outcome not normally forthcoming. In less fortunate cases, after repeated efforts to explain the situation, we develop an uneasy feeling that something is basically wrong, not merely with the symbol but somehow with the symbolizer, with our opposite-in-argument.

Of course, we have accepted our opponent at the beginning as both intelligent and honest. Otherwise, we would not be fraternizing with him even in friendly argument. But as this initial assumption suffers attrition from his obstinacy, we quickly enough come to suspect that he is not as intelligent as we thought—certainly not as intelligent as we are. So we redouble our effort to convert him, suffering such frustration, meantime, as to raise in us almost inevitably the final suspicion that our opponent is simply not honest —not intellectually honest at least. He *must* see what we mean, must see it but will not admit

it. Intellectually dishonest, he finally is not entitled to further explanation, which will prove
unfruitful anyway. So at last, through normal
development, often covering much elapsed time
and more frayed patience, we either agree to
disagree, puzzled into admitting the radical ambiguity of our symbols; or we resort to more
drastic measures, taking at length the easy way
with dissenters.

The undertow which leads sectarians to this
eventuation guarantees a place for a *diabolus* in
almost every system of divinity. It is a poor
deity who does not have his "opposite," and a
rare disciple in whom does not ferment this
malign egoism. If there were not a devil, deity
would have to invent one in order not himself to have to represent this "devilism" of the
saints. (Plato, it will be remembered, forbade
all imputation that God was the author of evil.)
It is a pity that every religion does not enshrine
the sly forbearance of the modern Hindu philosopher who declares that "every sinner should
be allowed a future, as every saint has had a
past."

The pass, however, to which religion historically conducts is not forbearance, as Maimonides
lets us see in the foregoing case of Ibn Tumart,
the Mohammedan conqueror. But the logic involved, and its wretched outcome, are unfortunately not confined to Mohammedanism, or to

any one religion. Wherever we meet this attitude toward ambiguity, its weakness is obvious
and organic. What such logic lacks is the very
core of what we mean by the ethical: its weakness is the absence of disinterestedness, and in
the end the utter loss of magnanimity. It was
his clear seizure upon this radical flaw in man
that made Thomas Hobbes's refutation of his
critics as lethal as it was laconic. In one devas-
tating sentence the old materialist answers three
classes of his pseudo-idealistic critics: "That [1]
I made the civil power too large, *but this by
ecclesiastical persons;* that [2] I had utterly
taken away liberty of conscience, *but this by
sectaries;* that [3] I had set the princes above
the laws, *but this by lawyers*" (italics added).
Hobbes claimed that all disinterestedness is pre-
tense, for a purpose; his critics demonstrated, as
touching themselves, the sad truth of his indictment. This is precisely, too, the fact which leaves
immoral this logic of presumption, wherever it
be found. Whoever arrogates to himself the cus-
tody of the unequivocal invites exposure, however pious his pretensions.

I do not myself suppose that this flaw of character is by any means confined to theologians.
No man escapes the undertow of the primitive;
and any incorporation of men, in whatever name,
accentuates the downward pull felt by individual men. But the modesty of secularism

affords partial catharsis. Whoever admits that he is not God has an initial start on modesty. There is something peculiarly odious about the dark impulse which religious men surrender to in defiance of all their claims of brotherhood.

I must ask them, therefore, to be as charitable as they can be while I indulge, as touching their anomaly, in a candor to which they are not accustomed. Good taste in intellectual matters should allow give and take, whereas we in America have approximated the position where religion is exempt from criticism; men of God may "give it" but need not "take it." We will presently see who can, and who cannot, measure up to holy reciprocity.

If what I am about to say does hurt anybody's feelings, I shall be sorry; but I beg him, in the charity which he professes, to remember what he so self-indulgently forgets: that his presuming a corner upon the noble impartiality of self-preference has often hurt my feelings. Indeed from my boyhood on the open plains of Texas up to a manhood now past its prime, I have been deeply, grievously, and continuously offended by the claim of sectarians to a preferred access to spirituality, a near monopoly claimed in the sacred name of God.

Sir Winston Churchill illustrated, during the late war, an attitude which commends itself to all independent minds. King Saud, of Arabia,

whom Churchill was formally to meet, expected,
as his right and because of old custom, full prerogative for all his prejudices. He did not
smoke, and men should not smoke in his presence; he did not drink, and men should not
imbibe before him. Churchill did not see, nor
do I, why presumption should always have first
lien on prerogative. Turn about even as to
presumption would seem to be fair play. So the
doughty Englishman let it be known as counter-
presumption that "my rule of life prescribed as
an absolutely sacred right smoking cigars and
also the drinking of alcohol before, after, and
if need be during all meals."

That, surely, was but to even accounts—and
it was allowed by the Mohammedan! "His own
cup-bearer from Mecca offered me a glass of
water from its sacred well, the most delicious,"
continues the good-humored winner slyly, "that I
had ever tasted."

All waters are sweet to the taste when drunk
by men who have met upon the level and will
part upon the square.

Before turning now, closer to home, to Catholic and Protestant examples of the logic of
presumption, let us take a Jewish case in pre-
Christian times. Its logic will lead us directly
to its duplication in Christian theology.

iii. *A Jewish Example*

I resist the temptation to parade the way the
Jewish community in Holland perpetrated upon
Spinoza and others of their dissident sons the
same logic by which the Christian Inquisition
had liquidated the Jews in Spain or had driven
them to Holland. I pass by this example in order
to emphasize an Old Testament text which par-
ades the self-same logic of presumption.

"The fool hath said in his heart," runs the
familiar text, "there is no God." Now as a matter
of historic fact some fool may indeed have said
precisely that. Fools are many, and they say
many things, wise as well as foolish. I asked a
Negro chaplain on a troopship from Europe, at
the end of the Second World War, whether he,
too, thought that there were no atheists in fox-
holes. After long reflection he admitted that it
was probably so; but he added, "It is not the
kind of religion I'd like to have to depend upon
in civil life." Some fool, I repeat, may sometimes have affirmed atheism; but that is a far
cry from what we have in this text—namely, the
conclusion that one who disagrees with us on the
question of theism is a fool. To utilize that logic,
to call one's brother a fool, because of any difference, is to get in smelling distance, says Jesus,
of brimstone.

Yet that presumptuous conclusion is precisely
the one drawn by the Jewish psalmist in the

passage alluded to. The quotation concludes, as
against all atheists: "They are corrupt, they have
done abominable works. . . . They are all gone
aside, they are all together become filthy; there
is none that doeth good, no, not one."

When I scrutinize that logic, I recall not only
the condemnatory words of Jesus; I bethink me
also of the noble and heroic life, before the
American bar, of my old friend Clarence Darrow,
and of many a village atheist whose names have
often led communities in deeds of mercy. Such
stridency of judgment as this Jewish maxim invokes, the harshness of branding a man a fool
because he disagrees with us over the reference
of a symbol, albeit the sacred symbol "God," is
prelude—as who does not know?—to the conclusion that the man is dishonest; and this is
prelude to the eventual withdrawal, through
fanaticism, of the full rights of fellowship, if
not of citizenship, from those who have flunked
so loaded a test of honesty.

Down this road lies the easy way with all
dissenters. Let the invocation of Jesus of "hell
fire" upon those who call a brother-in-argument
a fool be now applied prospectively to all Chris-
tians who depreciate the doctrine of the founder
by the invocation of such narrow logic. Jewish
or Christian, Catholic or Protestant, it is all the
same definitely and downright immoral, forget-
ting that one himself is not God, to insist in an

argument upon being judge when one is also defendant. It is this logic which makes proselytism so easy an imperialism of the spirit.

IV. *The Catholic Problem*

Characteristic of the Moslem culture, because it was and perhaps still is unashamed of the sword, and discernible in Judaism, which has at times been spiritually xenophobic, this same logic of presumption finds easy residence in the Roman Catholic sector of Christianity, devoted as is the Church of Rome to order as an end and un-averse as it is to authoritative definition as a means. The old doctrine of Papal Infallibility, become nineteenth-century dogma and operative upon all believers under restricted conditions, relieves any guilt the individual communicant may feel for the practice of such logic and enables the Holy Father himself to ignore the difference between himself and God, by making him the Almighty's vicegerent, God-on-earth. Protestants and independents may smile at such corporate conceit, and all free heads may nod— as did Lord Acton, the Catholic historian—at the thought expressed by Justice Holmes (a remark I once had the prized privilege of quoting to General Douglas MacArthur in Tokyo) to the effect that the happiest day of his own life was the day he discovered that he was not God!

This, however, is no laughing, nor even smil-

ing, matter to most Catholics, so organic to
their faith is this logic. Such corporate infallibility makes effective, no doubt, with a minimum
incidence of guilt over its presumption, the
machinery already branded in Mohammedanism
and Judaism as downright immoral. Note now
how indigenously the logic prevails throughout
the vast domain of the Roman Church. All the
illustrations which ensue follow logically from
two simple dogmas admitted, I believe, by all
Catholic apologists: (1) that the Church judges
as to *what is true*; and (2) that what is adjudged
error *has no rights*.

St. Thomas, the philosopher of the Church,
takes the easy way with certain dissenters
through the dominance of this double faith. Of
such heretics he declares, in the *Summa*: "So far
as they are concerned, heresy is a sin by which
they have deserved not only to be separated from
the church by excommunication but also to be
put out of the world by death." Pope Gregory
XVI invokes the logic against tolerance in what
can only be described by outsiders as a holy
tirade (the encyclical *Mariri Vos*): "That such
absurd and erroneous opinion, or rather that
form of madness, which declares that liberty of
conscience should be asserted and maintained
for every one."

Father James A. Ryan (with his collaborator
Millar) mollifies the universal logic into Ameri-

can exacerbation when he sweetly invites the prospective victim of the logic gracefully to preside at his own funeral. Says Father Ryan, in a passage which should not be as surprising as it is to some American Catholics (since it but voices the common faith):

A Catholic State could not permit other [communions] to carry on general propaganda nor accord their organizations . . . exemption from taxation. *While all this is very true in logic and in theory* [italics added], the event of its practical realization in any State or country [shades of Franco!] is so unlikely that no practical man will let it disturb his equanimity or affect his attitude toward those who differ from him in religious faith.

I never read this passage from Father Ryan, as audacious as it is disingenuous, without recalling Joseph Grew's judgment on the outrageous Japanese statement about China: "China refuses to show sincerity!" "Henceforth," observes Grew to that, "I shall always hate that word [sincerity] because it will remind me of the Japanese connotation of it: if I hit you and you hit back, you are obviously insincere."

Hear the same logic put to rhetorical use by the mellifluous Bishop Fulton J. Sheen:

America, it is said, is suffering from intolerance. It is not. It is suffering from tolerance. . . . The man who can make up his mind in an orderly way [can even make up his mind to let somebody else make up his mind for him?], as a man might make up his bed,

is called a bigot; but a man who cannot make up
his mind, any more than he can make up for lost
time, is called tolerant and broadminded.

Only the communists have hitherto sensitized us
Americans to such blatant doubletalk.

The victim of such logic, whatever its source,
should make himself ready for "supreme unction"
when he permits the official voice of any church
to make a virtue of the vice of narrowness. A
man who will undertake the cure of the ambiguous by simply lopping off the generous faith
of his betters in tolerance, declaring the virtue
of intellectual scrupulosity to be mere slovenli-
ness—such a man, albeit a bishop and a tele-
vision star, has already reached in his own mind
the end of the fateful road down which such
logic always points.

In order to suggest how prevalent in theology
is the acceptance of this logic of presumption,
I have now dipped for illustration into various
levels of the Catholic hierarchy, historic and
contemporary: from a philosopher (Thomas), to
a teaching cleric (Ryan), to a popular contemporary bishop (Sheen), via the official voice of
a pope (Gregory XVI). This logic is bad enough
when it is thus consciously recognized and so is
mitigated through limitation of area (as in the
dogma of infallibility). The logic is even more
lethal where it is held without being recognized
and where it therefore operates without limit.

Quite typical of lay impercipiency (in America, where anti-clericalism does not operate as brake upon applied presumption, as it does in Europe), is an article in *Look* magazine (January 1954). Mr. John Cogley, a lay Catholic, was invited to discuss frankly "The Catholic Problem." He touches on many "problemettes," so to speak—and touches on them nicely, too—but of this logic, the only "Catholic problem" really worth remark by intelligent Americans, he shows himself so oblivious that one can only guess in truth that he is utterly unaware of the moral bearings of the Church's high-handed way of presuming upon honesty no less sterling than its own: there is no will of God, save *our* interpretation of it; there is no natural law unless it says what *we* say it should! It is hard enough to be dismissed at all by fellow-men, but to be thus dismissed *inadvertently* invests the injury with an atmosphere of insult. How is it possible to be good friends, however much friendship be desired, with those who settle your fate without the courtesy of consultation? "To work hard, to live hard, to die hard, and then go to hell after all—would," says Carl Sandburg, "be too damn hard!"

The very best mitigation which such logic allows, under Catholic auspices—and it is far from good enough—is what Archbishop Paul Schulte of Indianapolis disclosed in his reply to the Spanish Cardinal Segura's outburst against an economy of tolerance. The American cleric's brave reply is picturesquely entitled "The Cardinal Is Calling the Cops Four Centuries Late."

In time, [says the American Catholic] we trust even the Spaniards will recognize that although religious error has really no rights, the heretics who hold the error do have certain fundamental rights which the state must respect.

This is not enough, for it really holds securely only for a non-Catholic state. Each time reassurance is given, it turns out to be less than complete assurance of toleration in all circumstances. The Catholic weekly *Commonweal*, for instance, has recently called attention to the words of the Pope, who has laid down the following two principles: "First, what does not correspond to truth and the moral norm objectively has no right either to existence, to propaganda, or to action. Second, nevertheless, in the interest of a higher and broader good, it is justifiable not to impede this error by state laws and coercive measures."

Even this assurance, however, is based upon a "nevertheless." And this adversative foundation is spelled out in the Jesuit fortnightly *La Civiltà Cattolica*:

The Roman Catholic Church, convinced, through its divine prerogatives, of being the only true church, must demand the right to freedom for herself alone, because such a right can only be possessed by truth, never by error. As to other religions, the church will certainly never draw the sword, but she will require that by legitimate means they shall not be allowed to propagate false doctrine. Consequently, in a state where the majority of the people are Catholic, the church will require that legal existence be denied to error, and that if religious minorities actually exist, they shall have only a *de facto* existence without opportunity to spread their beliefs. If, however, actual circumstances . . . make the application of this principle impossible, then the church will require for herself all possible concessions. . . .

In some countries, Catholics will be obliged to ask full religious freedom for all, resigned at being forced to cohabitate where they alone should rightfully be allowed to live. But in doing this the church does not renounce her thesis . . . but merely adapts herself. . . . Hence arises the great scandal among Protestants. . . . We ask Protestants to understand that the Catholic church would betray her trust if she were to proclaim . . . that error can have the same rights as truth. . . . The church cannot blush for her own want of tolerance, as she asserts it in principle and applies it in practice.

That would seem to be something like the final word, in clarity and in disingenuousness. Injury is not to be taken as an insult when the perpetrator thereof is committed to the injury on principle. The meager mitigation which each succeeding statement of the principle seems to carry receives in turn complete cancellation from the Church itself, which proclaims ever and anon through its "inspired" voice what Leo spells out unambiguously in the encyclical *Libertas*

Humana: "There is no reason why genuine liberty should grow indignant, or true science feel aggrieved, at having to bear the just and necessary restraint of laws by which . . . human teaching has to be controlled. . . ."

Whoever sports such logic consciously, or sustains it the more lethally because unconsciously, invites adverse judgment upon his ethics by all free men, who claim for themselves only rights they grant others. Nor is it defense against bad conduct or an evil will that the doers or harborers of the evil believe in a deity who commands it. Instead of imputing provincialism to God, genuine men of God will impute it to themselves and absolve themselves as best they can for harboring a logic which is a drag upon their ethics.

Even, however, if no harm at all were ever done to anybody in the name of such presumption, the logic itself is intrinsically immoral. That is our main case: it is bad per se to believe such things. As to the likelihood of injury to be added to the insult, let the wise remain watchful. It is disingenuous, even when candid, for sectarians to claim that the logic of presumption will not produce an ethics of infliction. It is so far forth a credit to most Catholic spokesmen, as almost every present citation shows, that rather than denying victimage to non-Catholics (as can in varying degrees be seen to prevail in Spain, and even in Italy), they seek to prepare the victims

to accept in "the right spirit" what will normally
befall them, come the "Catholic state." Protestants and independents cannot really say that
they have not been alerted to, even while being
softened for, their fate by Catholic thinkers.

Indigenous as this logic is to, and pervasive as
it is of, historic and contemporary Catholicism,
it was not initially from the Catholic source that
America learned its constitutional lesson, and
got its irresistible inducement to separate once
and for all from power those who espouse, with
whatever mitigation, this dangerous logic of
theology. Difficult as toleration was, America
early was promoted from the level of toleration,
whatever the source, to the highland of free
conscience. Not from Catholic, but from Protestant, perpetration came our first illumination.
America suffered a sovietism long before the Russian brand arose. The latter is a soviet of Marx-
ian sinners; ours was a soviet of the Puritan
saints. The saints taught us what we have to
fear from all exponents of the logic of presumption. The Puritans drove our independent fathers
beyond the negative logic of toleration, in which
it is assumed that somebody knows the truth
but will not inflict it, into a positive logic of
the free conscience: (1) everybody knows the
truth, or (2) nobody knows theological truth;
and so, either way, (3) everybody stands religiously upon equally admissible foundations.

This is the doctrine of free conscience as distinct from the doctrine of the erroneous conscience, assumed by toleration. Where consciences are free, there is nothing to tolerate anybody about, and nobody is constituted to be invidious enough to tolerate anybody.

v. *A Protestant Warning*

Roger Williams, it is sad to recall, was persecuted in Massachusetts "for conscience' sake." So he said, in his appeal for British justice against American Puritan provincialism. Those who had come to this country to find freedom for their consciences drove him out of the colony, he alleged, because he insisted on following faithfully his own conscience. The reply was at hand, as in the previous cases of un-Christian logic used against Christian ethics.

No, argued John Cotton, we did not drive you out, as you "aver," for following conscience; we drove you out because you refused to follow conscience and do what you well knew to be right. There it is, all over again, not merely making victims of independents in Massachusetts, but driving Quakers to Pennsylvania and Catholics to Maryland. The exact words of Cotton will bear quoting: "The erroneous party suffereth not for his conscience, but for his sinning against his conscience."

This fixation upon finality will return to the dogmatist in spite of all his efforts to be reasonable. It is like the story of the man who got an obsession that he was dead. All went on as before save his constant reiteration that he was a corpse. When a committee of friends waited upon him to argue him out of the fixation, he reminded them that though he was indeed talking to them, nevertheless it was a dead man who was doing the talking. Having extorted from him an acknowledgment that "a corpse never bleeds," they asked his permission to put him to the test by slitting his wrist gently with a razor blade: no blood, he was indeed a corpse; any blood, he was a live man. They slit his wrist as agreed, and as he watched the blood trickle out, he looked up at his friends and exclaimed disarmingly, "What do you know—a corpse *does* bleed!"

Against such a background, it was to the root of the logic itself that our fathers laid the axe of exorcism. They saw that the gravest immoralities would, in America as in Europe, be committed in its name as long as that logic had access to power. Foolproof indeed the logic is; but nobody save a fool or a fanatic would resort to it. Ethics forbids a wise and good man to stoop so low as to conquer anybody with the weapon of an ex parte definition. The wise and the good will admit that ambiguity, even in theology, is not merely a fault of language, to be blamed off on heretics, but reveals, so to speak, a cosmic "fault" to begin with, and constitutes an eventual doorway to wider meanings for such as are exercised thereby.

Queries Thomas Jefferson of the mania for sameness, which underlies the logic of presumption: "Is uniformity attainable?"

"Millions of innocent men, women, and children," he is forced to answer, "since the introduction of Christianity have been burnt, tortured, fined, imprisoned; yet we have not advanced one inch toward uniformity."

The only "advance" which Jefferson could recognize was, as he put it, "to make one half the world fools, and the other half hypocrites."

Then inevitably must the previous question be obtruded, the question as to the ethics of such logic: "But is uniformity of opinion desirable?"

The answer is simple, final, and radical: "No more than that of face and stature."

So Jefferson broke through the barricade of presumption. He boldly advised a nephew, his ward, to "question the existence of God, because if there be one, he must more approve of the homage of reason, than that of blindfolded fear." And completely separating opinion from action, he declared of theological opinion: "It does me no injury for my neighbor to say there are twenty gods, or no God. It neither picks my pocket nor breaks my leg." Thus he not only emancipated opinion from the narrowed options of action; he pointed to the generous path which ever invites the footfall of pilgrim feet. Negatively, it drove him to declare as his opinion that "history furnishes no example of a priest-ridden people maintaining a free civil government." Positively, it drove him to universalize knowledge of God, if there be knowledge, or of ignorance, if ignorance prove the lot of man.

A logic which involves all religions alike in guilt, as we have seen (and the stronger, the guiltier), must have deep roots in order to maintain itself against such prima-facie ethical indictment. That the rootage of this logic is egoism—corporate in Mohammedanism and Catholicism; individual in Judaism and Protestantism—is clear for all to see who wear not the blinkers of utter sectarianism. Hobbes not only admitted it for himself; he proved it against those who denied it most vehemently. But such crass derivation of fanaticism from egoism does not seem sufficient to shame sectarians into moderate generosity of judgment.

The deeper rootage of such presumption is in the will-to-power, deeper and broader than egoism. But something is wrong with the countervailing will-to-perfection when it surrenders so easily to the solicitation of power. The deeper explanation is, we suspect, to be found in the

notion of truth which obtains in sectarian circles.
Any notion of truth is justly suspect which im-
putes "error" to every other man's way of seeking
the truth. A doctrine, that is, which awards
logical purity only to oneself, and which grants
logical immunity to none but oneself, cannot
be appropriated to oneself with ethical impunity.
This abstract theme we shall pursue in the last
chapter.

It is not that the Catholics are by nature worse
than other sectarians. They are only worse by
logic. They punish themselves more than most.
Others have to resist only the undertow of primitivism; they must resist the very tides of virtue
itself. Let us say it more in sadness than in
censure, but let us say it unambiguously: Catholics sport a logic which insulates them, and
then they blame their isolation on those whom
they make equally the victims of such alienation.
They are officially committed to circumvent the
simple decency of good neighborliness. Our
complaint is not merely against peripheral in-
felicities, such as the papal denial in America
of Rotarian membership to the faithful or such
as the papal refusal in England to let Catholics
join with Protestants and Jews for enhancing
ordinary amity; our complaint is against something organic, the central war which Catholic
logic carries on with Christian ethics. It is indeed
hard to be at ease with those who connive at

your damnation, however reluctantly they follow
the bent of their own logic in doing so.

All theology, as we have seen, feels the undertow of this lethal logic. But liberal Judaism has
emancipated itself from ungenerosity in accepting the notion of a developing deity. Protestantism is saved from the worst of fanaticism by the
multiplicity of sects. If anybody starts the bully-
ing business, every Protestant fears he may get
gored in the melee. The Protestant necessity of
allowing tolerance as sheer prudence has at
length superinduced a feeling of more than
tolerance as the pervasive protestant principle.
In Catholicism the logic of presumption joins
hands more fully than in other cults with an
always too available will to power. The logic
of presumption tempts all orthodoxy, but this
proves fatal to only those who have or who
aspire to get and use state power for sectarian
ends.

Says the great Catholic sociologist Mercier,
"Crime is the result of temptation offered to
temperament." The logic of presumption is ever
a temptation to undercut decency in judgment.
In their ordeal of grace, however, Catholics constitute but a special case of the general rule. Said
Justice Holmes—speaking like a judge for the
generality—"Persecution for the expression of
opinion seems to me perfectly logical. . . . If you
have no doubt of your premises or your power

. . . you . . . naturally . . . sweep away all opposition." And we may add that, if you *do* have doubts, this logic may make you all the more trigger-happy, in order to show yourself that you are not really tinged with dubiety! A wise man has described the fanatic as one who redoubles his energy as he forgets his goals.

Sectaries could relax their special case of hardship by allowing themselves the leeway provided by a logic of generosity. Truth may not be as narrow as sectarian minds impute. Such metaphysics as could fraternize with morality would be a gracious thing. We would here plant the seed, and later cultivate its soil, the thought that no immoral conviction—not even the most sacerdotal conviction that one himself has a corner on truth—can ever be adequately defended on merely logical grounds. Generosity as disinterestedness is prerequisite to safe logicality. This thought we shall allow to lie fallow for a time, until we can call in the politicians to ease the social tensions engendered by religious sectarianism. That is what politicians are good for. The extremity of sectarians may provide just the opportunity for the diplomats. Meanwhile, as the theologians cannot seem to surmount ambiguity with charity and band themselves together for heaven, we shall keep them loosely herded together for whatever other destination their dissidence may prescribe on the docket of fate.

2. The Ethics of Democracy

We have done now with the negative aspect
of our subject, the misuse made of ambiguity in
the name of piety. There is also a use, a large
and noble use. In the next chapter we shall be
climbing from the present lowlands of politics
to the axiological heights of philosophy—steadily
and ever climbing. In the present chapter, however, we must locate and assess the techniques
of man's collective life.

Politics is our wisdom of the beginning, but
it is not any proper ending for aspiration, as we
shall see. Political accommodation exists for the
sake of the spiritually uncompromisable. Politicians do know what to do about ambiguity—
and what not to do. There are, however, three
kinds of politics, having their common source in
the problem of dissidence reflected in the phenomenon of ambiguity. We must distinguish
among these three.

1. *"Strategic Obfuscation": Cure of Ambiguity*

Politics of every sort arises indeed from the
temptation—a temptation too heavy for sectarians to sustain—to regard one's brother-in-am-
biguity as a knave or a fool. If you succumb to
the temptation and call him a knave, you beget

on earth, as far as you can, the equivalent of
the theologian's hell: the shocking geo-politics
of fascism. If you succumb and call him a fool,
you beget on earth, as far as you can, that other
equivalent of the theologian's hell : the wretched
neo-politics of communism.

We dare thus to relate provincial theology and
authoritarian politics on the safe if humorous
advice yesteryear of the dean of a great divinity
school (it was Shailer Mathews, of Chicago)—
the advice, namely to conceive theology as
"transcendentalized politics." The power game
is indeed little different, whether indulged in
heaven or played out on earth.

There is, however, in addition to geo- and
neo-politics, *a democratic type,* though with little
chance, I presume, of getting "transcendentalized" into any heaven where sectarians would
feel at home. At any rate, we must first win to
democracy on earth. The initial need is to get
the democratic type sharply set apart from the
kinds of politics that share with theology the
logic of presumption in seeking the resolution
of ambiguity.

Let us the while keep close connection with
our home base of symbolism by identifying politics at once as the art of "strategic obfuscation."
All ambiguity is obfuscation, and frustration, too,
for one whose only goal is clarity. As all of us
do at times seek clarity, all of us are sooner or

later caught in the web, either as doers or sufferers, of obfuscation. Theologians and philosophers indulge in it, however unintentionally and unwillingly; politicians accept and even practice obfuscation both willingly and intentionally. They do it "a-purpose." Politicians are unafraid of ambiguity because they recognize it to be a "given" and they know its prepotent use. They treat it as an end as well as a means. As a means it must be adjusted through compromise. But it is doorways to ends that are variegated and lustrous. Says Thomas Jefferson, the arch-politician, "If no varieties existed in the animal, vegetable or mineral creation, but all moved strictly uniform, catholic and orthodox, what a world of physical and moral monotony would it be. . . . It is a singular anxiety which some people have that we should all think alike." So Jefferson expected differences at the end as well as at the beginning of every political process. But in between he knew uncannily how to use political means for ends that were not political and were superior to things political.

Just as the theologian uses the ambiguous term "will of God," and the philosopher the ambiguous term "natural law," and then each denies that *his* term is ambiguous, so the politician uses a term like "justice," but in full knowledge of its slipperiness. He *has* to start with the ambiguous; for he begins with individuals or groups at each others' throats, each demanding justice but each requiring of the politician something different—fortunate if not something downright *contradictory*.

Why, we do not even name the accommodative process "politics" until all techniques designated by happier names—"friendship," "fellowship," "comradeship," "sportsmanship"—have been found wanting in relevance or in effectiveness. The politician, we repeat, is forced to start with warring factions, each claiming a monopoly upon the value symbolized; and his success from that enforced and inauspicious beginning is measured, negatively, by the degree to which he can prevent an ex parte settlement of the issue, and, positively, by his reconciling both or all actors to such varieties of thought and feeling as justify, as well as necessitate, a common mode of action.

The very fact of ambiguity taxes the politician's creative powers to contrive a formula which, because it *does* mean different things to each side, may stop the quarrel, with the semblance of sameness, and may enable the factions to proceed peaceably. "The only path of *orderly* change," observes Thurman Arnold, "is through a confusion of principles. Clearcut and logical systems suddenly imposed bring the violence of Russia, Germany, or the French Revolution."

The art of accommodation—invidiously called

"compromise"—is thus the very crux of the politician's power to arrest, if not to cure, the malaise of ambiguity. Seeing this, let us now clear up and render as acceptable as possible this whole inevitable confusion of principles called "compromise": the authentic nature of compromise, its context and the limits of its availability in making ambiguity creative. I know as well as any that "compromise" is a term of ill repute. But I know why; and, knowing why, I see that there is no utility, or courage, in trying to substitute a term more palatable; for the substitute, when put to the same inevitable but distasteful use, will suffer the same declivity of reputation. ("The statesman," you know, "is but the dead politician.")

It is only impetuosity which cannot abide ambiguity; and with impetuosity the peacemaker must be quit, like a youth done with childish tantrums. Since, then, any other symbol would be corrupted by the required function, let us further explain the nature of compromise and then seek to purify its context, if possible, and thus to arrest the chronic depreciation of perfectly honorable symbols. The context in which civilized men practice the art of compromise reveals both the necessity of its utilization and its desirability, but discloses also its limitation as a final principle. Ethically, we shall find compromise superior as a means, inferior as an end.

II. *The Nature of Compromise*

Compromise is the process, then, whereby each party to a conflict gives up something dear, but not invaluable, in order to get something which is truly invaluable. In the very nature of the case, therefore, compromise is a sacrifice exacted particularly of "good" men, a sacrifice which their very goodness requires but renders odious. One of my undergraduate students has well stated the ambivalence of its incidence by describing compromise as "the lowest of the goods but the highest of the evils of collective life."

What we need to add now, before turning to consider the context of compromise, is that in its very nature compromise involves "principles" no less than "interests." It is an easy distinction, and very satisfying to the tender-minded—the distinction between "interests" and "principles." If we can somehow feel that in paying the price for accommodation we never trench upon the precincts of our souls, then conscience rests back upon its oars, without feeling the guilty price of the final exertion. This final exertion—we may even say exaction—is, in the business of politics, the giving up of something which to us involves "the principle of the thing." This I do not wish to overstress, for I too make, and indeed up to a point honor, the distinction between "principle" and "interest." I myself, as will plainly appear presently, exclude from compromise all the mat-

ters of "first rate" concern. But, placing oneself
inside the orbit of a given option, it does appear
that conscience gets tinctured if not tainted in
the grave business of thus adjusting interests-in-
conflict. Men do give up in politics—this is why
the practice is so hard on idealistic constitutions
—what seems to them in part at least high principles.

To understand this fully is to see why politics
is not a dirty game, nor politicians either stupid
or dishonest (though of course it takes all kinds
to make a Congress). What adverse value there
is about politics arises not chiefly from bad men,
but from good men—men who insist in the name
of their consciences upon being good in a unique
way, namely, each in his *own* way. At its easiest,
and for the most part, politics is of course the
adjustment of economic interests in conflict.
Were this all, politics would be easy indeed, and
relatively unimportant. James Madison saw
(*Federalist Papers*, No. 10) that this is prime,
but he also saw and emphasized that economics
is not the worst basis of human dissidence. "So
strong," says he, "is this propensity of mankind
to fall into mutual animosities, that where no
substantial occasion presents itself, the most friv-
olous and fanciful distinctions . . . as well of
speculation as of practice. . . . have been sufficient to kindle their unfriendly passions and
to excite their most violent conflicts."

Conscience is indeed a flexible and growing thing even when we mean to keep it static. Men will invest, as Madison has said, their most meaningful concerns with the sacred mantle of "oughtness"; and, as they do so, what was yesterday but an "interest" becomes today a "principle," a principle on which one cannot yield without some sense of guilt. But while this is happening to one side, the same thing is happening to the other side, even in economic adjustments. Pending a later extended illustration of this involvement, we may now salt down the suspicion that in every great conflict of interest, the "principle" (of justice, let us say) is somehow involved.

Since both sides suffer some guilt in trenching upon ideal justice in their compromises, and since guilt festers unless aereated, it is in the nature of the case that both sides will objectify for the aereation their guilty feeling, fixing it upon the nearest appropriate object. Near enough for blame always stands the politician, as representative. He who arranges the compromises becomes easily enough the double scapegoat of this natural and dual transfer of guilt. This works well enough as long as it does not get out of hand by the refusal of the parties involved in the compromise to abide its guilty terms or as long as it does not get under the skin of the politician himself, giving him gastric ulcers or throwing him upon the trash pile of "tired liberalism" or, worse still, heaving him upon the dung heap of cynicism.

Says Mr. Charles P. Taft of contemporary politics: "This I would state as the decisive issue: How does a person, either as responsible follower or leader, adjust his conscience to the requirements of team operation in the face of complex issues and proliferating organization . . . ? How does a responsible leader know what is the essential principle which he may not concede, and which point is incidental, or at least may be deferred without serious damage?"

Having said this much upon the ethical component in the make-up of compromise, let us further appreciation of this type of political accommodation by observing now the larger context in which the good work goes forward.

III. *The Context of Compromise*

The necessities of compromise are laid in our very frame. Life is an equilibrium of energies, few of which can trespass upon others without causing illness and none of which can monopolize the field of the organic without risking death. The history of therapy attests the necessity of interorganic accommodation, from the earliest blood-letting to equalize the humors on down to the very latest advances in sociosomatic medicine.

As physically we exist by constant redress of disparate urges, so the mind lives upon prowess preserved against the prevailing of any of its separate elements. The too imperious encroachment, for instance, of the dream upon action spells insanity, and the too successful resistance to the dream turns man into a clod of utter practicality or into a beast of unshamed passion. The life of the mind is a succession of "flights and perches," as William James described it; or it is, with Hegel, an antithesis posed to a thesis and saved from imbalance by a synthesis happily indigenous to its changing seasons; or the healthy mind is conceived, with the older and ever wise Plato, as reason, the royal charioteer, driving in unity a team that taxes ingenuity by struggling against each other while also assisting and resisting the wise mastery of the charioteer.

When this interorganic and intramental accommodation shows itself in social life, it spells compromise in a sense more literal than the adjustments we have only now remarked. Men are diverse in interest, and they are not always harmonious in principle. The extent to which any one interest can be made totalitarian and dictatorial, even in the simple field of the economic, is limited by the division of labor requisite to the survival of any ample population. Workers of brawn cannot wholly deny rights to workers of brain, or the reverse, without cutting out from

under each side its own support. Healers of
souls cannot entirely deny healers of body without finding themselves shy of souls to save, nor
yet preservers of the bodily equilibrium deny
with impunity lawyers, as surgeons of social dis-
equilibrium, the right to a standard of life com-
parable to their own. Here, as elsewhere, the
necessity and the desirability of compromise run
together and issue as a single stream.

It is this convergence that makes an ethical
enterprise out of politics, which is the institu-
tionalized art of compromise; that makes the
politician the official custodian of consciences
borne by men too weak to sustain them socially;
that invests the legislative process with the accolade of moral midwifery. If men cannot practice compromise themselves, they become victims
of its practice upon them by others: for its practice prevails, willy-nilly. It prevails even where
the overt alternative to it appears to have won
the day; it prevails, that is, under dictatorship.

In the struggle which goes on inside the "elite"
or "gang," constituted by the dictator and his
advisers, there is always give-and-take. Where
this is not so in the beginning, as perhaps with
Hitler in connection with the Russian campaign,
it is so in the end, as with Hitler and his advisers
after reverses in Russia. These inner struggles
over the determination of direction and subsequent distribution of either the spoils of victory

or the bitter spoilage of defeat—these struggles illustrate the compromise game in the camp of its enemies, albeit the game played irresponsibly, as now in the Russian hierarchy. Compromise is, indeed, a necessary derivative of finitude. Only infinitude could circumvent its necessity. And playing at God leaves man nearer the devil than before, for it swells his normal human weakness into presumption through the poison of conceit.

There is, however, another and more pathetic sense in which dictatorship, as a would-be alternative to a compromise-economy, itself illustrates adversely the compromise principle. In so far as the dictator has his complete way without compromise, he wreaks his will upon the wills of others. They knuckle under, finding "compromised," in the worst possible sense of the term, not only their economic interests but their dearest moral convictions as well. Compromise will out, either as totalitarian murder or as the essence of democratic morale.

Advanced peoples elect it as morale. That is the reason that they are advanced, and that is chiefly what constitutes advancement. Civilization may, indeed, be well conceived as the social process wherein men elect to do their own compromising, thus keeping the process responsible and making its results the ripe fruit of victory rather than the rotten refuse of defeat. When

men elect in tolerance to meet each other halfway, they promote the practice of compromise
from the lowlands of irresponsible odiousness
to the high level of moral creativity.

It is this creativity of democracy which has
led some of its students to object to "compromise" as the term to describe the principle of
accommodation which it uses. But this is a short-
sighted lead, as we have seen. The derogation
of the symbol arises from a deprecation of the
function. Conscience cannot escape from the
corrosion—if it must be held so—of compromise.
Only soft-headedness will have it so.

We have seen in our time what such softness
means internationally. When men have grown
accustomed to interpret their duty as the practice
of benevolence alone, they find themselves utterly unprepared for handling the malevolence
which intermittently dictates man's duty, if man
may think it a duty to survive. Pacifism is the
logical outcome of an ethics of aspiration that
makes no place in itself for evil. But pacifism is
pusillanimous in the presence of those not im-
pressed by the noble principle of non-resistance.
I have heard an eminent religious pacifist—it
was John Haynes Holmes—declare that the
meaning of religious conviction is the faith that
a good man cannot be put in the position of
having to choose between two such evils as, for
instance, to fight on the field of battle or to be

mutilated in the concentration camp. Are there, then, no good men in China, in Czechoslovakia, in Poland?

This romanticism of faith when reduced to secular foundations may divert the meaning of compromise away from conscience and exhaust it in adjudicating conflicts economic. Any scaling down of economic claims, especially of the other fellow's claims, is eagerly accepted and lauded as legitimate compromise. So it is: such compromise is entirely worthy of the esteem given it. But any encroachment by the legislator upon what the high-minded critic regards as the domain of his conscience is at once censured, and the censure is generalized in the conception of the politician as scapegoat, "the low compromising fellow!"

This narrowness of vision arises in part from the fact that high-minded citizens are usually concerned with interests that do have a superior claim upon legislators—education, for instance. Superiority of claim does not, however, mean finality of merit or exempt the superior conscience from compromise. Men who espouse such good causes must be prepared in dispute to meet somewhere near halfway those who as honestly think that another diversion of taxes (or limitation thereof) is the right thing to legislate. The poor and helpless hold politicians in more esteem than do the educated and privileged,

whose concerns have become vested interests
which are rendered sacrosanct by a premature
taking of concerns as foregone.

Prematurity does not constitute finality, and
moral certitude of the educated and the sensi-
tive falls far short of certainty in the democratic
way of life, where "each counts for one and nobody for more than one." I must insist that the
context in which compromise arises is such as to
render suspect all claims of conscience to preferred consideration. The limit of compromise is
not fixed beyond all doubt, by an appeal to conscience; and any conscience that thinks so becomes by that very fact an apologist for a covert
form of privilege.

There is a special claimant, if not indeed a
little totalitarian, hidden in the bosom of every
conscientious man, especially if he be a middleman operating in the name of God; and the conscience that does not see itself as a power drive
needing sublimation through politics is perhaps
more dangerous to democracy than the conscience that crassly admits that it means to have
its way regardless. "Rationalization" is the bad
meaning already achieved by intelligence which
hides behind conscience, giving forth "good"
rather than "real" reasons for its preferred claims.
The context of compromise is two-fold—non-
moral and moral. It is the inexorable conflict of
interests among men which most easily marks

the domain and enforces the technique of compromise; but it is the fact that there stand on
both sides, as parties to all the great conflicts,
men equally good and equally determined to
see that goodness is not shamed by those who
are blind to it, which equally distinguishes the
domain of compromise. Where equally honest
and equally intelligent men espouse what, for
all that finitude can see, are equally legitimate
interests, wrapping conscience around opposite
sides of each controversy, there economic interests get compromised, if they do, only at the
cost of conscience itself. Conscience either compromises or gets compromised.

The way in which politicians, who arrange the
major compromises, are made the scapegoats
of nearly all conscientious men, lends high prob-
ability to this accounting of what happens in the
career of conscience as a would-be innocent by-
stander to social conflicts. Men unable to face
what amounts to a semi-betrayal of their principles without loss of self-respect pass the buck
to the scapegoat and through projected blame
save themselves from loss of face and, but for
that, loss of liberty also. By such devices partisan claimants of the good win time in which to
educate their consciences to the acceptance of
the best that can be achieved collectively as
foundation enough for their self-respect. This
accounting makes it possible for us to see com-

promise as moral, in a sense downright creative for the collective enterprise, and educative for individual lives. Compromise is, indeed, the process through which, given the machinery of guilt-transference, conscience itself grows more and more robust. The conversion of the provincial into the socially adequate requires time, patience, and strategy. There is no pain like the pain of a new idea, especially if it be novel to conscience. In this larger context of patience and strategy we may see compromise as the very principle of growth, whereby conscience passes continually from approximate fanaticism toward a roomy worldly wisdom. Civilization is, indeed, always "beyond conscience," as I have suggested in a book of that title; but it is a "beyond" that is "within"—well within the magnificent pattern of human competence.

Let us now legislatively illustrate both the necessity of all-out compromise and its beneficent results before passing to the more analytic task of disclosing its limits. Consider a perennial drive, coming to a recurrent head in Congress, the drive against (and for) a national wage-and-hour law. This drive, pro and con, is mercenary on the surface, but only on the surface. The shortness of the work-week seems to some to reduce output below the level of safe profit, not to say below the level of national security. When efforts are made to retrieve this loss and to

increase production by overtime, the wage pro-
vision doubles the profit-hazard: time-and-a-half
for overtime and not unlikely with wages doubled
for Sunday and holidays. Mercenary on the
surface, the drive is deeply moral at heart, in-
volving consciences on both sides.

Assuredly, in the light of all the factors involved, it is disingenuous to doubt the sincerity
and sustained honesty of manufacturers and bus-
inessmen and of their elected voices in Congress.
This honesty is complicated, though not im-
pugned, in the South, whence its loudest voices
arise, by a sincere agrarianism and a deeply felt
resistance to the collectivization of labor which
industry threatens to bring in its train. In both
South and North the drive is further complicated,
if not purified, by the sentiment of patriotism
which prevailed at the inception. How can
labor loaf along, the patriots ask, on forty hours
a week, when their, as well as our, sons are at
the command of conscription if not at the door of
death twenty-four hours a day, seven days a
week, on the sea, on the land, in the air? And
how, in heaven's name, they persist, can labor
haggle over time-and-a-half when our boys and
our allies, deprived of arms or ammunition
thereby, thus have their own hazards doubled—
and that at a trifle of peacetime pay? A profit
motif is here, before our very eyes, transformed
into a moral cause pregnant with patriotic fervor.

This is a transformation, however, that, unfortunately, is no respecter of persons. Now let us look at the other side of the conflict.

The drive which enacted this statute and seeks to sustain it is also mercenary on the surface, but only on the surface. The unequal access to leisure in a civilization dedicated to equality of opportunity has long been a shame. The shame was deepened by what has seemed to be the collective impossibility of remedying the sister shame, the grossly unequal purchasing-power in a civilization with an ever rising standard of living. Why should not the men who do the body of the world's work reap "their share" of what they create, and, failing that, why in heaven's name should they not be compensated by a larger leisure in a world where more and more is created by less and less? Clearly labor was out to get, and clearly is now out to keep, its largess in our expanding prosperity. Mercenary on the surface, this drive, too, is deeply moral at heart.

For why not—why not indeed?—labor with its wages swollen to absorb the ground swell of our national prosperity, or, that failing, with its leisure enlarged to pass the work around and to share the major psychic income from toil? Why not, indeed? Is democracy a moral enterprise dedicated to equality of access, or an immoral one dedicated to monopoly of enjoyment?

And as for patriotism, who in the last war was it that identified patriotism with profiteering? Is this "gang" now to be allowed to make patriotism the second refuge of scoundrelism, economically speaking? Thus the hidden thoughts of certain laboring men and the strident pleas of their audible voices in Congress. And, as for forty hours a week, let management, let bureaucracy, show that *they* are producing more. Let the efficiency experts testify at what minimum number of hours the maximum output begins to decline. Call the statisticians to testify whether there is a shortage of labor, save at the level of such high skill as will not be helped by increased hours or lessened pay. And, last of all, look at the marvelous morale reflected in labor's voluntary renunciation of the strike (and even of doubled pay for holidays) for the duration of World War II, and at the remarkable speed with which we bettered even the German record at converting our nation into a full-bodied war thrust.

It would surely be picayune to doubt the sincerity and morality of laboring men and of those who defend the convictions of labor in the Congress of the United States. This honesty, like that of the other side, is complicated, though not invalidated, by many factors. But it is confirmed by one enduring fact, the fact that democracy is a moral impetus ever making for equality among men—first for political voice, but at last for the economic access of all to the rich margins attendant upon an age of science. War, or peace, for democratic ends is a sounding brass or a tinkling cymbal unless it is furthered by men sharing in its prosperity as well as in its hazards. This, after all, is what the shouting is all about, or ought to be about—a materializing of the ethics of equal access.

These two sides, with swords flashing but with arguments seldom neatly clashing, confront each other in Congress in every recurrence of the agitation over hours and wages. Each side has a material stake, but one which has been heavily moralized; and each cause alike continues drenched in patriotism during a period of the cold war. Equally honest men, with causes equally sincere, meet in such manner that neither of them can permit the other to have its way without loss of face and impairment of self-respect. That's politics, as met and practiced in the context of legislature or Congress.

Such a case will but recall to our democratic minds a double fact: the fact, first, that there is no other way of settling such issues as justly as by compromise; the fact, second, that such settlement requires the presence of a third party. Such settlement is politics; such a third party is the politician. This path of compromise is indicated to avoid dictatorship and death, and it is desirable as a means to set each claimant on the way to such uninflamed memories as will facilitate neighborliness in the conduct of future business.

Compromise, then, it would appear, arises in the narrow context of social necessity and functions in the expanding context of individual growth and social progress. By transmuting the necessary into the desirable, men of good will make some minimum freedom of their inescapable fate. Only in utter privacy of a conscience devoted to contemplation or of a consciousness contentedly otiose would there be no necessity of compromise. Every step taken from that blissful state of solipsistic anarchy is taken "by your leave," "you" being any other soul with whom I elect to associate without either arrogance or condescension.

In groups that are small and like-minded, associations which one joins and which he can leave when he likes, there need be but a minimum of compromising, because there arises only a minimum of conflict. But, as one increases the range of action, he decreases the amount of uncompromised autonomy. At last, in politics, where rules are for all, they can be made only by give-and-take; and even through that method the amount of one's higher ideals that can be made to inform a statute is ordinarily very low indeed. The reason you cannot, to any large extent, make men moral by law is that moral men cannot agree on the meaning of what is moral or what law would be conducive thereto. Good men disagree as to who is to make whom do what. Lucky is the society whose laws represent a level of ideals somewhat higher than the lowest common denominator of individual consciences. Luckier still if, while bad men stay "within the law" thus lowly laid, good men exemplify in their individual actions ideals that are well beyond the level of the law. To demand the maximum of ideality at law is to achieve the minimum, for the impetuosity of such demands involves dictatorship as the method of accomplishing it. Such insistence suppresses the consciences of all but the dictator and his own compromise-clique.

As testimonial, therefore, to a statesman-like view of our second topic, the context of compromise, we now enunciate two principles of social life, if you will, in relation to ideals—the one a sheer necessity of peace, the other a basic condition of progress: (1) *The quantity of compromise required in society varies directly with the area of action;* and (2) *The quality of ideality surviving compromise varies inversely with the size of the collectivity.* The relation of the two to each other may best be seen if we force them into one formulation: *Quantity and quality of ideality for action vary inversely.* A great moralist of our time, Nicolai Hartmann, was driving at this truth when he declared that the higher the ideal, the weaker, and the lower, the stronger.

To demand the maximum of ideality—the highest demands of the private conscience—as the rule of collective action is to suffer the minimum of ideality; for, since other consciences will never wholly agree with the highest vision of any conscience, this vision can be put into action only by coercion, which in turn outrages all other values and mutilates its own by the form of implementation indulged in. To settle collectively, on the other hand, for the minimum of ideality is to facilitate the private realization of the maximum. This is so because the minimum can be agreed upon; the agreement establishes an atmosphere of peace and permits each conscience to go back to its groups of likeminded people and there work out its highest promptings unpolitically, for the subsequent improvement of a body politic more sympathetic to one's ideal demands.

To apply, for instance, the top demand of the conscience of either labor or capital to the conflicts between them would be to provoke either strikes or lockouts, which in turn would inflame both sides to an adamant insistence upon the impossible; whereas for each to accept as a working basis what little the other can allow is to create an atmosphere in which both may, in one way or another, approach nearer their maxima.

Nowhere is it truer than in the career of conscience in society that he who saves his life shall lose it, and he who loses his life shall find it.

iv. *The Limits of Compromise*

A principle which, like this of compromise, is both necessary and desirable in social life would seem to be applicable without limit. Shall we, then, proclaim the main business of life to be compromise? Shall we, indeed, spend our time in nothing else than discovering more and better ways to compromise? Shall we greet our neighbor each morning with the friendly challenge: "Hast any compromise in thee this morning, neighbor?"

No, compromise is not applicable to life without limit. By way of indicating three limits to compromise, let me begin with a waiver: compromise does not apply to the individual in his privacy. Make nobody else's business your business and you will never have to do business with compromise. Containment, as we shall see, is insurance against compromise. Stay at home and you will escape the inevitable rigors of the road. But who wants to stay at home forever? So this brings us to our first general limit.

(1) This limit is necessity. A man does not have to compromise with himself, and so the good man does not do so. We have argued that in social life, however, compromise is a neces-

sity. Sometimes it is, and there we indulge it.
We have argued that compromise is desirable.
Sometimes it is not, and there we do not indulge
it. Where compromise is not necessary, it can
hardly be desirable. Whoever, indeed, goes
about hunting up chances to sacrifice his interests is a masochist, and whoever hungers to
sacrifice his principles, if there be such a speci-
men extant, is a pervert. Sacrifice, which genuine compromise involves, is a virtue only where it
is a necessity, and its virtuousness reaches little
farther than its necessity. Whoever will let others
run their interests over his own is a "sissy," and
whoever will let the conscience of another out-
weigh his own in the bargaining process is a
"softie." Necessity, then, is the mother of compromise, and we present the necessary as the
first boundary of our principle.

Not all that bristles, however, is necessity. In
the competition of interests, bluffing is an established game, just as, in the competition of principles, we have seen that presumption is an
established technique. Men must be wise as
serpents if they are to become doves harmless
to their own rights. Men wisely compromise
when they are deadlocked, since none of the
other alternatives involves as little sacrifice. As
compromise is desirable only when necessary,
so now we affirm it necessary only when somehow desirable. Desire, however, also functions

quite as much in a field of narrowed option as in a freer field. Men will accept a half-loaf, but only when they are in need of bread and cannot get a whole loaf. There come times, nevertheless, when men prefer to do without bread altogether rather than pay the price of even a half-loaf. It is under such conditions that we approach the second boundary of compromise.

(2) This second limit is peace. Not all that woos our desire wins our wills. Compromise, when necessary, is desirable upon the assumption that the sacrifice involved will not lead to other sacrifices ad infinitum. Since compromise is an alternative to war, it loses its cause for being if it does not lead toward peace. Sacrifice for the sake of larger and larger sacrifices makes no sense. The prospect of peace with progressive lessening of sacrifice is the goal whose absence marks the limit of the action.

If men prefer strife to harmony, compromise is neither necessary nor desirable; and if men are put in such impossible conditions as to prefer the risk of death—and even death itself—to complicity in conditions resulting from sacrifice, then compromise has reached its limit, and its opposite will appear to us as the most desirable evil open to option. Where the choice is between definite goods and easy evils, compromise is opportune. But where the choice is between definite evils, compromise grows hard, though still tolerable if one evil is clearly less than the other. When, however, the evils are arduous and yet the choice inescapable, the compromise principle grows creaky of operation through cautious circumspection. If the evil offered is intolerable, leading to certain struggle with the effective means of further successful struggle forfeited, then compromise has reached its second limit; for to make the sacrifice would yield no peace in which to recoup.

This limit of tolerability is most surely marked by intolerance itself. We can tolerate without limit the tolerant alone. Intolerance always warns us of the encroaching limit where fighting must supplant the accommodation of compromise.

Munich has become the current international symbol of a condition that recurs universally. Chamberlain compromised with Hitler, or thought he did, by sacrificing Czechoslovakia. He brought home what, had it proved less than illusory, might have well rendered the sacrifice tolerable for Englishmen, and possibly in the long run for the Czechs—he brought home, as he said, "peace for our time." That, however, was only upon the assumption that Hitler was compromising with him by sacrificing something of his own. It soon became evident that Hitler expected Englishmen to be tolerant of his aims but that he did not mean to tolerate theirs or those

of anybody else. When it became obvious that
Hitler was all "take" and no "give," the resulting
situation itself became intolerable: Englishmen,
seeing the price paid and no peace ensuing,
preferred war and the risk of death to further
toleration of an attitude eventually intolerable.
If intolerable eventually, better untolerated now
while some means are left for effective struggle
to right the wrong which has already been allowed.

Munich is the destructive symbol of compromise out of bounds. The Bill of Rights is our
constructive symbol of compromise within
bounds. I say "within bounds," because there
is abroad in the world and even among us a
misconception of what the Bill of Rights charges
for what it guarantees. This we shall make more
clear in the concluding chapter; but it is appropriate to say here that it guarantees freedom
of *private* conscience from compromise only
upon the acceptance of compromise as the peaceful settlement of all *public* disputes. Politics,
we repeat, is the undisputed king of all that is in
final dispute. If, when men get into serious argument, they agree that the word of the mediator
supersedes the dictates of private conscience
upon that matter, they thereby guarantee the
peace and take as their privilege, in return, complete freedom of belief, a very large amount (the
larger the better) of freedom of speech, but only

such freedom of collective action as is collectively approved.

The theory of the constitution is that the politics of compromise alone makes possible the peace in which no compromise is required. Otherwise such freedom is impossible, because freedom of conscience violates freedom of conscience. Only where conscience agrees with conscience can conscience proceed to do fully what "ought" to be done, even in the name of religion. A Cook County judge, under provocation from a belligerent sect, has ringingly declared against insolent trespass of the privacy of home in the name of religion:

Hurtful meddling with the souls and minds and religious beliefs of others is obnoxious to the very spirit of our federal and state constitutions and was not meant to be safeguarded by their guarantees for freedom of worship. . . . In their wisdom the Fathers foresaw that violent clashings of religions will ultimately crush all faiths in America as they did in other lands.

The principle of this decision is sound, as against trespass even in the name of religion, whatever the prudence of the decision in judging the facts of the sect in question (Jehovah's Witnesses). Conscience crucifies conscience on the cross of presumption unless the saints are protected from one another by political sinners who arrange the compromises of conscience and thus constitute the law which private citizens can agree to call "the public conscience." Over against the tendentious dictum of Hilaire Belloc, that "all political questions are ultimately theological questions," we must set the opposite conclusion, that all theological questions are potentially political questions. They can remain sacrosanct only by remaining private; the moment they are obtruded as questions of public policy, they lose their sheltered position, and become political questions to be settled, like all other questions in dispute, through the compromise technique of engineering consent.

Toleration, domestically as well as internationally, is for the tolerant alone. Men who will not tolerate other consciences and the law which protects all alike from undue interference, will not themselves justly be tolerated by the law, save behind bars where the law in a pinch puts such presumptuous souls. I have already spoken of "presumption" as an established technique in the prowess of conscience. A man who antecedently to conference knows all that is right has very little to teach others; for they will match with pride his own presumption and will refuse to learn from him who advertises that he himself has not learned the limits of what he knows. As Marchette Chute has so well said, "You will never succeed in getting at the truth if you think you know, ahead of time, what the truth ought to be."

A man, on the other hand, who has achieved modesty enough to admit that he is not God, is not going to permit some other man who has not made that discovery to interpose upon him a bogus finality of judgment. A man who does not respect other consciences by wooing them only with their consent, is not himself guaranteed freedom to exhibit his conscience in collective action. Complete freedom ends with utter privacy, and it tapers off toward action only by general consent. If we tolerate the intolerant, we do so as a matter not of their right but of our graciousness—and we do so within the limit of prudence, watching meantime for any sign of their will to trespass. Toleration belongs by right only to the meek. The downright intolerants deserve to get "socked," whether we always deserve to "sock" them or not.

(3) This brings us to the third limit of compromise. We add now to necessity and peace the limiting condition of progress. That there are compromises *and* compromises, life quickly teaches us. We can achieve peace at a price which quickly abolishes peace and yet makes it impossible for us to recoup what we lost through the effort. We have seen that Munich symbolizes this phenomenon. But we can also achieve peace at the price of stagnation, which, while not

intolerable, turns all things dynamic to the static. Compromise must not be made a mere adjunct of statics. It has in it the power to become the major principle of dynamics. But this prospect counsels us to set as its final limit the possibility of progress. Compromise between two equally tolerant and dynamic persons or groups is not doomed to point down and down to death through acceptance of the intolerable in the name of peace; it can point up and up toward unlimited progress through mutual accommodation.

The possibility of progress is the dearest possession of our Western way of life. Modern democracy arose, indeed, when men could inscribe upon their banner the "perfectibility of mankind." Science was young in the seventeenth century, and its hopes were high. Science is ambivalent with maturity now, and hope is lower; but the period of hopelessness has not yet set in, nor need it arrive soon. Where two or three are gathered together in any name, and can stay together, there arises out of their union a new strength with its own instruments of potency. If we pay the price of keeping together, we may compensate for the sacrifices which are entailed. Progress is the compensation which compromise furnishes and furthers.

When compromise is made upon such conditions that the sacrifices required to perfect it will breed further sacrifices at the next stage of compromise, then the compromise principle has met its third and final boundary. Renounce all hope, ye who dare this boundary. This is the place to quit compromising and to begin to fight, with fuller faith in revolution than in evolution foredoomed to devolution. Contrariwise, if the standards of life, or merely the state of feelings, can be so promoted by this compromise as to warrant that the next compromise will require less inequality of sacrifice, then we are operating inside the third boundary which safeguards the fertility of compromise.

Progress, however, is a slippery term—even more slippery than the names given to the other limits: "necessity" and "peace." The chief ambiguity that should now be guarded against is the one which narrows its meaning to the economic or even to the external. There is a state of feeling which is no less fecund for civilization than is a given standard of living. Indeed, it is arguable that the chief task of our time is the internalization of that external thing heretofore called *laissez faire*. With frontiers gone and vast spaces conquered and exploited, the amount of external freedom which is compatible with large populations is more limited than previously. When *Lebensraum* is not available for the incautiously fecund without depriving the less fecund of the fruits of their circumspection, what brand of justice is it that will give the fruits of caution to the incautious?

If the Germans, for instance, had been willing to internalize their demand for *Lebensraum* and to find fulfillment for the demand in an intensification of their culture, they might have won some lasting triumph. If they had been willing to furnish to civilization men more skilled and more cultured than other countries could furnish and to take as their reward a growing deference to what is finely Germanic, it is possible that they could have achieved more than they have ever achieved, or will ever achieve, by the crasser standards of their extraverted will to power. Other peoples could then have met them halfway and in so meeting could have so mellowed their Prussianism that the result might have seemed, even to them, full justice. *Lebensraum* of the spirit is something vastly different from the literal demand to blow your beery breath into the face of every foreigner you meet.

Flouting peace, however, they made such demands upon more civilized men as would have converted compromise into appeasement and would have turned the clock of progress back an unpredictable number of decades. Since the world could not make such compromise seem compatible with progress and since Nazi peace meant what civilization had always understood as war, the Germanic determination to use necessity, apart from all desirability, illustrates our major law of ideals—that to demand the maximum ideality collectively is to achieve the minimum, whereas to accept the minimum offered through compromise is to be on the road to more and more progress.

Let not all this emphasis upon compromise, in its context and under proper limitations, obscure from us our simple initial fact: that the life of compromise is not the end, but only the means, to spirituality. The collective aspect of democracy—for which compromise is the key—is subordinate to the personal aspect. Containment is superior to compromise. The individual is the be-all and the end-all of the democratic way of life. The life of the spirit is highest and best beyond the realm of political accommodation. It is, we repeat, the uncompromisable which compromise exists to safeguard.

This large double aspect we wish now to reduce to the concreteness of an American example: that of Abraham Lincoln before the fatal issue of slavery. The question was otherwise than "to compromise or not to compromise"; the question was *how* to compromise so as to honor the means which accommodation is, and yet safeguard the ends which accommodation serves. How to stay within the limits of fruitful accommodation? Lincoln's story will properly close this chapter on the practice of compromise, and as properly introduce the final chapter on the high art of containment.

Because he knew what he did not know, and was modest before his ignorance, Lincoln was hardly more the preacher than the ardent practitioner of the art of compromise. He practiced it in marriage, to preserve domestic peace; he practiced it in the Cabinet, to maintain party unity; he sought to practice it in diplomacy toward the South, in order to preserve, and later to restore, national union.

Had he, like Daniel Webster, been at the time an idol of the people, he would, like Webster, have been castigated and cast out for accepting the nauseous fugitive slave compromise. Whittier said of Webster in his elegy of damnation:

> . . . From those great eyes
> The soul was fled:
> When faith is lost, when honor dies,
> The man is dead.

Even the gentle Emerson said, more bitterly still, of Webster:

> Why did all manly gifts in Webster fail?
> He wrote on Nature's grandest brow, *For Sale*.

Even in his relative obscurity, before the presidency, Lincoln did not escape his cup of castigation. A contemporary abolitionist paper described him as a "middleman, between a very modest right and the most arrogant and exacting wrong." And a later disparager of his compromise role has put it ironically: "If the wind comes my way, I have set my sail for it; and if it does not come my way, it is not much of a sail I have flung forth, and not dangerously noticeable."

Nor is Lincoln's guilt without witness, any more than is Webster's. Both men indeed pleaded guilty of compromise, but with extenuation. Admits Lincoln:

> If slavery is not wrong, nothing is wrong. . . . Yet I have never understood that the Presidency conferred upon me an unrestricted right to act officially upon this judgment and feeling. . . . And I aver that . . . I have done no official act in mere deference to my abstract judgment and feeling on slavery.

With clear understanding, that is, and with right feelings, Lincoln nevertheless condoned, or at least participated in, the odious wrongness of human slavery.

Nor was Lincoln's role in the famous debates any less "compromising" than that of Douglas, hero worship of Lincoln to the contrary notwithstanding. They both proposed compromise as the cure of the national ambiguity, though their proposals were differently attuned to the facts. Lincoln, like Douglas, would compromise with slavery *where it was;* but he, unlike Douglas, refused to compromise with it, so to say, *where it was not.*

In the territories, Lincoln would permit no ounce of compromise. "No line dividing local from federal authority, nor anything in the Constitution, forbids the federal government to control as to *the fruits* of slavery in the federal domain." And as to Southerners, defenders of slavery and beneficiaries, "They are just what we would be in their situation. If slavery did not now exist among them, they would not introduce it. If it did now exist among us, we would not instantly give it up." And, in general, "wrong as we think slavery is, we can yet afford to let it alone where it is."

Ready as Lincoln was to practice compromise, as a second best, he almost seemed at times equally ready to preach it up as the very best. I say "seemed" advisedly; for Lincoln never actually forgot the deep line which separates action, where we do the best we can, and thought, where really good men always know better than they do. Speaking of the Missouri Compromise, Lincoln said, in a famous speech at Peoria:

The Missouri Compromise ought to be restored. . . . Restore the compromise and . . . we thereby restore the national faith, the national confidence, the national feeling of brotherhood. We thereby reinstate the spirit of concession and compromise, that spirit which has never failed us in past perils, and which may be safely trusted for all the future.

Clearly there was nothing else to trust; but, more clearly still for this juncture, that trust was not enough. It is nothing to the discredit of the spirit of accommodation if men failed of heroism to sustain it. Men of principle in the North could not sustain the spirit of compromise; and, at length, men of principle arose in the South who could not sustain the ordeal of conscience. The moralist's extremity became the politician's opportunity, but an opportunity which was fated to fail on the very shoals of adamant principles. Both sides got beyond the grace of containment. All went down over the rapids together. Later Paul Laurence Dunbar wrote, of another occasion:

> Once in the river of ruin,
>   What boots it, to do or to dare,
> For down we must go
> In the turbulent flow,
>   To the desolate sea of despair.

Lincoln, standing on the edge of the precipice, clairvoyant of the flood which would come after the failure to compromise, declared in his First Inaugural:

Suppose you go to war, you cannot fight always; and when, after much loss on both sides, and no gain on either, you cease fighting, *the identical old questions as to the terms of the intercourse are again upon you* [italics added].

This chapter closes with the sad sunset of the spirit of concession. The next chapter opens long before dawn, in the sickly darkness which Lincoln foresaw. War always makes more necessary what for the time it renders impossible. Compromise stays for containment of conscience.

3. The Art of Containment

With the breakdown of compromise between the states, war came, as conflict always follows failure of the spirit of concession in the face of strident ambiguity. Once begun, war deepens the crisis of spirit which provokes it; it hardens principles, it narrows options. To reinstate compromise—and there will still remain no other course—is harder after than before a war, as Lincoln so clearly foretold and as his successors found out. Magnanimity is made more difficult, but more indispensable, by the very fact of fighting. The essence of the title of this final chapter is this spirit of magnanimity which Lincoln commemorated in saying that what he dealt with was "too vast for malice." This we shall now spell out in extending the Lincoln illustration from compromise to containment.

With some three hundred and fifty thousand dead in the North and a hundred and thirty thousand in the South; with both sides impoverished in purse and neither side softened in spirit; with every slave (of the conquered states) "emancipated" but with not one Negro really freed—with all this, "the identical questions," as Lincoln had predicted, "as to the terms of intercourse" were once more before our fathers, North and South alike.

Moreover, the ambiguity as to the metaphysical nature of the Union, which they could not handle before the war, they could not handle after the war. Magnanimity sufficient to liquidate the war was made inoperative by the fact of the war. Martial history, as John C. Calhoun once said, always makes "the error of yesterday the law of today." George F. Kennan adds, in *American Diplomacy: 1900–1950*, "Every mistake is in a sense the product of all the mistakes that have gone before it, from which derives a sort of cosmic forgiveness; and at the same time every mistake is in a sense the determinant of the future, from which derives a sort of cosmic unforgivableness."

Abraham Lincoln gives us the best example extant of how to mitigate this historic guilt and to lay hold upon the cosmic forgiveness. Just as wars of theology had been compromised by holding the Christian God to be *both* one and three, so a way must be found through the *e pluribus* to the *unum* of the states. This old quarrel as to the nature of the Union came to a post-war head, of course, in the problem of Reconstruction. Lincoln had tried his hand at the hard matter in an experimental program for Louisiana, a program characterized by ambiguity but charged with leniency. It had, nevertheless, worked fairly well (a fair failure is always moderate success, following a war) in a single state, and was now up for extension to others of the conquered states. But of course the war had left a legacy of heat, not light. Lincoln had been attacked in Congress for trying to reconstruct the peace, as it were, without having settled the cause of the war. He would pacify the South, said his enemies, without clarifying the principle that had made Southerners rebels. Had they or had they not been out of the Union? Were they or were they not to be brought back into it? That was the metaphysical question.

Lincoln admitted that he had not raised that sixty-four dollar question; he declared that he would not raise that question; and he concluded that to raise that question would make more pressing questions unanswerable, the more so after than before the war. "That question," he said simply, "is bad as the basis of a controversy, and good for nothing at all—a merely pernicious abstraction." Lincoln's insight (it is to be found in his last public address, two days after Appomatox and three days before his assassination) is final and remedial.

The moral for us we must now draw. That question, said Lincoln, "could have no other effect than the mischievous effect of dividing our friends." The trouble at the end in the North was the same trouble as between the North and the South at the beginning: it was a vast ambiguity. "We, the loyal people," declared Lincoln openly, "differ among ourselves as to the mode, manner and measure [of Reconstruction]." Well, that is indeed the root of the difficulty: we always do differ, somewhere, somehow, "as to the mode, manner, and measure" of whatever impends collectively.

Carl Sandburg, Lincoln's biographer, illustrates this human predicament with a humorous bit of folk wisdom. "Don't I argue? Don't I sputify?" the backwoods preacher inquired of the complaining committee, whose chairman responded, "Yes, you do argue and you do sputify but you don't tell wherein!"

How to deal with specifics—how, that is, to turn human differences to dynamic account, rather than to let them operate as something lethal—brings us back to our previous problem of ambiguity and prepares us for our denouement of self-containment. To generalize the problem of dissidence, and to summarize now what we have been about from the beginning, let us lay it down anew that not all good men are ever wholly agreed on goodness; not all just men are ever wholly agreed on justice; and, particularly, not all holy men are ever wholly agreed on holiness. What are the consequences of these facts? As to justice, we usually manage to compromise, when we are both wise and lucky. On holiness, we usually turn our backs on compromise and run toward fanaticism, if not smack into it. As to goodness, this is our golden opportunity, if we can understand the art of containment sufficiently to advance from a narrow to a generous conception of truth.

By containment we mean simply what Lincoln did and what he recommended in the foregoing illustration that we do. He kept to himself his ultimate reasons for acting, and recommended the same restraint to all. Reasons are often different for doing the same thing, and sometimes the same for doing different things: keep your mind, then, upon what is agreed and hide in your heart what is in difference. Principles which divide men are, when obtruded, "merely pernicious abstractions," however sacred they may seem to fanatics. Such principles must be "contained," not perpetrated, for there is no peaceful public *lebensraum* in which to indulge them. However, this art of containment unfortunately belongs only to stalwart men.

Character is required to keep "oughts" to oneself, and a vast natural piety is indispensable as an antidote when felt obligation tempts one to a course of conduct that is coercive in promise. Nothing is more trigger-happy than a hyperthyroid conscience. Lincoln gave the final constructive touch to this matter in a quotation which we earlier truncated for emphasis. Let us now atone for that license by italicizing the hitherto omitted portion. "Wrong as we think slavery is, we can yet afford to let it alone where it is *because that much is due the necessity arising from its actual presence in the nation.*"

Here is broached, though not named, the natural piety which conditions and rewards the containment of ideals whose obtrusion can only deepen enmity. Certitude is never enough in dealing with ambiguity; sincerity only begets enmity when it is claimed without being at the same time granted. The consequence of obtrusion is grave—is war; the reward of containment is as great as the obtrusion is gravid. This reward is spiritual self-sufficiency. If all will forego baneful obtrusion, says Lincoln of the issue around Reconstruction, then "each forever after [may] innocently indulge his own opinion." This is mighty reward for mere laryngeal quiescence: to have as one's very own, and innocently to hold, such treasures of conviction as tend when released to interrupt communication and to poison all amity. In the precious fact of *certitude* we all have the power for good of an atomic bomb held in reverse, but the power for evil of the same bomb detonated.

We have now only to spell out the full meaning of the Lincoln illustration in order to pass, with the lonely man of Illinois, through the valley of sectarianism over and beyond the mediocrity of political compromise, into the vast reaches of spirit where compromise is left behind through the gracious practice of the art of containment. The final faith of the politician is just here: it is that some conflicts over principle can be composed. The faith of the *democratic* politician is that those conflicts which cannot be composed, can be contained.

I. *Certitude vs. Certainty*

This brings us to the beginning of the end. For this last lap of our pilgrimage we shall need to call to our aid the philosophers, long held in reserve, to help us now over the skyline pass which separates certitude from certainty. Out of deference to the presence of our friends, the philosophers, let us now, as they like us to do, distinguish between the near-and-dear role of our private convictions and the never-never land of infallibility.

The two realms are clearly not the same, though they alliterate easily and are often identified with each other by the impetuous. Certitude is but a candidate for certainty, a candidate whose greatest success is occasionally to be nearly elected. Certitude is what we "know" for ourselves as a feeling. Certainty is what we *know* with others for a fact. Certitude is a "given"; certainty is an achievement. The one requires no confirmation save our own consent to have it so. The other permits no confirmation save that of agreement: the agreement of the competent (in science) and the agreement of the majority (in politics). Certitude is private, individual; certainty is public, social.

There is a fatal tendency to run these like-sounding claims together without taking the pains to mediate. Ambiguity is always an index of this temptation. Those who take the shortcut with ambiguity are transforming their certitude into certainty without so much as a "by your leave." Those who take the longer, the round-about, way through scientific demonstration or through political accommodation may from private certitudes distil enough certainty to ground a measure of agreement sufficient for collective action. Certitude can be seen to be operative when, for instance, the late but not lamented Dr. Goebbels brought his mighty little fist down and declared with a resounding thump: "Jesus was not a Jew: it needs no proof—it is a fact!" Certainty is in the offing when W. K. Clifford declares: "It is wrong everywhere and any time, for anybody to believe anything upon insufficient evidence."

What we require, in order to overcome ambiguity, is either the grace to keep these two kinds of conviction apart or a legitimate way of getting them together. It seems impossible really to keep them apart, men being what they are. It is not impossible, under favorable conditions, to get them together. What we mean by getting them together, what we want as a final aspiration, is all the intimacy of certitude and none of the exactions of certainty. We want to eat our cake and have it, too: each to be his own Pope, speaking infallibly to himself upon questions of faith and doctrine, and yet each living in a peaceful society where we consult before we pontificate. Such ideal fulfilment is foreshadowed by what we experience in a like-minded group where nearly everything can be taken for granted. A universal community that is thus like-minded would give us a practical equivalent of the combination of certitude and certainty. Custom is such an equivalent in primitive groups. Why not then go primitive ourselves and quit debating about what, once doubted, is eternally debatable?

If we do not like such recession to primitivism, let us try the other option: the development of a self which is so sufficient that it can hold its certitudes without fudging them logically into certainties or without the appeal to authority which simulates universality of judgment in the face of natural dissidence. Too much dogmatism spells disaster for democracy. In this logic-and, nothing is ever a "must."

Now different fields of value are differentially fruitful for this high endeavor at certainty. Science, for instance, offers little scope for such preciosity, for science requires evidence and cannot rest short of what is hard at best: concensus of the competent. How arduous this way is, is illustrated by the professor of philosophy (theology) at Padua who told Galileo substantially that he would not look through the new telescope for fear that he would see a new planet which he knew was not there! Had either Aristotle or the Bible mentioned it? If that primitive way prove dishonorable for civilized men, then let them try politics as a method of joining certitude with certainty. But politics offers hardly more scope than does science for the indulgence of impetuosity. If you think it easy to get majority consent, you ought to try it out in some actual legislative body. Cocksureness is the enemy, not the friend, of majority consent.

Art, however, does offer scope. In artistic endeavor a man may maintain with certitude his notion of beauty without the certainty that what is beautiful for him is beautiful for all. "Aesthetic truth" allows deviation without the imputation of artistic "error." "Twenty men of genius," observed Justice Oliver Wendell Holmes, "looking out of the same window, will paint twenty canvases, each different from the rest, and every one correct. Life," says the Justice, moralizing, "is painting a picture, not doing a sum." From such a generalized observation, he concludes with this more overt moral: "Men may be allowed the defects of their qualities, if they have the qualities of their defects."

Religion is, or may be, a fecund field, theology apart. Religion offers, or could offer, vast scope to certitude, if the religious would not insist upon finessing certainty. All that stands in the way here is a moderate amount of ideological generosity. On such a showing, the opposite of what is religiously "true" for one devotee may be true, and certainly must not be branded "erroneous," for others. It is, as Santayana profoundly observes, the being ideal, not the being true, that makes religion the head and front of everything.

II. *The Leeway of Truth*

Since the problem of short-circuiting certainty seems to center around the category of truth, let us concentrate upon that historic ideal for a moment. If we start with the assumption that truth is so exclusive as to allow no neutral ground between it and error, we break up in a row as to what that exclusiveness consists of. "Whatness," so to say, wars with "thatness" — so much so that we can maintain the conviction of finality only by raising ambiguity to a permanent and an honorable status. There tend to be as many "whats" of truth as there are judges of its presence. Substantive absoluteness requires operative agnosticism to save the logical enterprise from debacle. To identify truth with one side of ambiguity is for truth to endanger its own *integrity*. It loses its career in the act of saving its life. If there is "scientific" and "artistic" and "religious" truth, have we not lost the substance of truth and are we not left holding only its semantic shadow? Yet if truth is cover for all that vastness called value, it must embrace all these divergencies—all these, and more.

The easiest way out of this ambiguity, which is so vast that it threatens to fritter all virtue away in vagueness of reference, would be to renounce the use of truth as the all-inclusive value-category and to identify it by definition with one meaning only. Candor might thus cure ambiguity. But that is the trouble, as we have seen, with the scientists, in the value field: not too much precision but too much exclusion. Still we might avoid their difficulty, if, dividing the whole field between many categories, we held them all to be equally honorable, as they are equally ancient. If we, for instance, define truth to mean only what has been demonstrated to the satisfaction of all concerned (the "concerned" being for practical purposes a political majority or those scientifically competent), we need not then, by the terms of the contract, hold that which is not true to be necessarily false. To do so would "falsify" all aesthetic and political and religious experience. And that is too much for even the rankest dogmatist to venture. He who knows not all these varieties of value argues himself unknowing of value.

If, however, we said that what of value is omitted in defining truth as the demonstrated, is contained under other value terms equally authentic, we would then have placed on a par with one another, but left ambiguous, the "good," the "beautiful," the "true," and—let us include for good measure—the "holy." To do this, I say, would appear to be the easiest way, if not *to* certainty, at least *toward* it. But what appears easy, logically speaking, is not always possible, humanly speaking.

So tenacious in the value field is resistance to generosity that one is driven to wonder whether ambiguity is not, over and above a logical necessity to be endured, a great axiological test to be treasured. It separates the men from the boys. "Necessary" evils are nearly always disguised goods. This suspected ambivalence we shall exploit positively before we conclude. Meanwhile, we must point out again the price of our indulging this human prejudice in favor of monism, which makes truth exclusive while making all that is excluded false. Such a procedure brands all deviation as "error" and lands us back where we started—with ambiguity as an evil to be exorcised, at first through intolerance and finally through fanaticism. The only cure left for this logical narrowness is a more generous ethics.

"But you do not ask us to desert our consciences and to sabotage our own sincerity—surely not that?" cries the sectary.

"That," we reply, "if we may state it more gently, *is* what we would hope, though hardly expect, seeing that it is your straitened self with which we have to deal. In truth, we want you to follow your conscience, of course; but we hope, with Ruskin, that it will not always insist upon being the conscience of an ass! Most assuredly, too, we want you to remain sincere; but sincerity need not be equated with sadism save in an agent who is mean."

Apart from education of taste, which is slow and not always sure, we may hasten the advent of a better ethics than fanaticism permits by stating once more, with the philosophers to help us, why the logic of presumption is personally inadequate and is democratically impossible. Nor shall we confine ourselves to the "push" of prudence; we utilize also the "pull" of beauty. The comeliness of virtue should constitute a more reliable appeal than the ugliness of vice. There is no moral magic in meanness; and, as touching religion, it still remains odious if not impious for men to worship a deity who is not as good as they are.

III. *A Moral from the Philosophers*

Let us now note the predicament of the philosophers, who are our specialists in dealing with axiological ambiguity. Since they, like the rest of us, start with what they have, they begin with the certitude of their own souls. The philosopher knows what truth is, and will tell you in no uncertain terms. Yet the state of philosophy in every free epoch will at once belie those bold words, "in no uncertain terms." Truth is so hard to come by, even for the philosophers, that "theory of truth" has become the great second best to truth itself for those who have dedicated themselves only to the best.

The contemporary quest *for* truth has in no small measure settled into the philosophic game of trying to checkmate the other fellow's theory *of* truth. For truth-seekers thus to divide hopelessly over both the definition of, and the practical approach to, what is sought—this is the order of outcome to which modern philosophy is largely reduced. Having myself no new revelation to give, let me but hand back the sad conclusion to which the philosophers have inclined me by their example, whatever their partisan claims. Surrendering scholasticism to theology, because of its dubious connection with sacerdotal power, we remark three current and independent theories of truth as testimony to the wry way in which the ambiguous dogs the tracks of the truth-seeker. Ambiguity becomes chronic "triguity" in the philosophic ordeal. Each effort not only disappears, that is to say, into a triune view of truth, but each emerges with a criterion for its success which is not available for finite minds (the only kind we human beings have). Note carefully what happens to the specialists who undertake to make truth so unequivocal that it can divide the field with "falsity."

(1) Coherence, one says, is the meaning of truth. But coherence is no adequate theory of truth. Only an absolute point of view could see that all things cohere, and such an absolute vantage is not available to men. What is not available can neither test nor be tested by finite frailty. Of this idealistic theory, then, I remark simply that it is only when men know not what to trust that they trust they know not what.

(2) Correspondence, another says, is the meaning of truth. But correspondence is no adequate theory of truth. One must know what is true before he can know what beyond his ideas corresponds with his ideas. Truth becomes, with the candid Locke, "I-know-not-what." Of this realistic theory of truth, then, I remark simply that it is only when men must say something that they say something which they themselves do not fully understand.

(3) Prediction, says the third, is the meaning of truth. But prediction is no adequate theory

of truth. If truth is prediction, then no idea is ever true, but is merely always about to be true. Prediction cannot *be* what it is *of* without compounding confusion. Since such basic categories are chronically confused, the inherent ambiguity of truth is likely to be tinged at times with comedy through errors of honest misidentification. Of this pragmatic theory I remark, finally, that it is only men who despair of truth who call prediction of it truth itself.

Having been thus sadly prompted to expose the inadequacy of each theory separately, I must now add my gravest doubt whether resort to "triguity" can mitigate ambiguity. The theories in part cancel one another out; and, more embarrassing, each theory in the joint effort fails to be an adequate test of its own truth. How, indeed, can coherence test the coherence theory? To what does the correspondence theory correspond? And what solvent prediction validates the prediction theory of truth? What appears to be the genuinely common element in all the theories, and what, I suspect, is that upon which reliance is actually placed as the only available test of truth, is some vague feeling of "all's right" which notifies the aspirant privately that things have "clicked."

Obviousness or self-evidence becomes the hidden resort, I am convinced, of all philosophical schools. Moreover, on this reliance, the schools merge quietly with common sense and unite in elevating "certitude"—*i.e.*, the oldest prejudice of man, the simple assumption that what strongly feels or clearly appears so, is therefore so—to the level of being the supreme test of truth. "The application of the adjectives true and false," says the logician W. E. Johnson, "coincides with the imperatives to be accepted and to be rejected, respectively." This softhearted conclusion from hardheaded logic is the reliance, it would appear, which sustains the faith in truth of the idealist (laboring with the ambiguity of coherence), of the realist (struggling with the ambiguity of correspondence), and of the pragmatist (wallowing in the slipperiness of prediction).

Now regardless of what may in each of us satisfy "animal faith," such natural dogmatism as is involved in the logic of self-evidence is plainly not enough for a scrupulous mind. Perennially appealing, this doctrine of common sense is pathetically inadequate as witness of truth, or as a substitute for it. Too much that is true is not self-evident (Einstein's General Theory of Relativity, for example); too much that appears self-evident turns out to be false (as the "obvious" flatness of the earth). "Certitude," says Holmes, "is not the test of certainty. We have been cocksure of many things that are not so." Indeed, to say that a judgment is self-evident does not mean that it is evident even to itself, for it is not a self,

but only an impersonalized judgment. And
surely the mere obtrusion of conviction does not
make it evident to other selves, especially to
those who at the very moment are disputing it.

As no logic is highly effective with an opponent when its major premise is that he is either
a knave or a fool, so no claim of self-evidence
evidences itself in the normal situation where it
is made, namely, in the presence of somebody
who disputes its validity. Sincerity, when thus
paraded as evidence of the truth only reveals an
impercipient mind or a brazen heart. Sincerity
is indeed a cheap commodity, at home or abroad,
when used as a wedge to cajole acceptance of
what otherwise lacks credence.

Nor does it remove the taint of logical cheap-
ness when, all other arguments having failed,
one rises and simply admits that his contention
is true, à la Dr. Goebbels. Let us, closer to decency, understand clearly that the very claim of
self-evidence normally arises only in a situation
that disproves the claim: arises, that is to say, in
the presence and because of the presence of
those who do not see it so at all.

"We hold these truths to be self-evident," said
our fathers—but only after they, having ex-
hausted arguments, had made up their minds to
fight. So the Declaration of Independence was
the declaration of war. That is the normal effect
of the resort to self-evidence in the presence of

ambiguity. To parade such adjournment of reason as though it were the final appeal to reason is disingenuously to demonstrate what we have earlier obtruded in all its pathetic nakedness, the logic of presumption as a poor cure for doubt.

Only certitude does self-evidence ever betoken —never certainty. And even the certitude must, like advertised coffee, be dated day by day. Moreover, the impasse reflected, and also intensified, by this claim, adds to the tragedy of trying for truth and never reaching it the deeper despair of spreading the fair mantle of truth over every hideous error and hellish intolerance since time began. Certitude reveals a logic-land where every man is king, but where no one is allowed by others to wear a crown.

Truth appears, then, not as an unambiguous symbol but as some vague clairvoyance of satisfactory relationship with an environment undefined if not illimitable in its scope. Little wonder that every intellectual formulation of this clairvoyance in a disputed situation proves specious in its clarity and illusory in its certainty. Less wonder, moreover, when we remember the reach in space and time of our total environment, cosmic and cultural.

Our human career is from elemental nescience through momentary prescience to ultimate nescience. The lights that flash across our little day of dim reason are lurid but lost in a sky of primeval and eventual darkness. Historic after-images get confused with premonitory gleams from a future rising out of the unknowable, like dawn from a night that is spent; and neither the after- nor the fore-images can clearly and surely be distinguished from the little glows of our own animal heats.

The result is that where we simplify value to a single symbol, like truth, we then must compensate the wrong done its fecundity with such a multiplicity of meanings for the unitary symbol that thereafter we can never tell for certain what meaning it is that we mean. If we start monistic, we end pluralistic; if we start pluralistic, we can work toward a monism of vagueness by persisting in the inquiry, "What is it that makes all these different values valuable?" The suitable nursery rhyme for us modern children of honest dubiety has already been composed by some unknown wit:

> Hickory, dickory, dock,
> The pluralist looked at the clock.
> The clock struck one
> And away he run—
> Hickory, dickory, dock!

> Hickory, dickory, do,
> The monist looked also;
> But the clock struck ten
> And he looked again, and said,
> "It is three hours slow!"
> Hickory, dickory, do.

Awakening from our childhood dream of omniscience, it is better, I think, to start with variety as one's datum, rather than have to end with it reluctantly, like one driven to his doom. The wise man is one who, with Spinoza, knows his limitations and, through acceptance, makes of his fate a vocation. To keep the jump on circumstance, even upon semantic circumstance, is a minimum freedom which cannot be taken away. Accepting this great trinity of ideals—inherited from the Greeks and seasoned through Christian centuries—we might regard them as equally honorable, adding to the trinity of truth, goodness, and beauty, a fourth, for fullest measure of plurality, holiness.

A metaphysics thus plural in its complexion will make ambiguity of symbols fruitful and will furnish us leeway to move naturally from one ideal domain to another when tensions require release. Idealistic tensions get heaviest in the sector of truth. The reason, or at least one reason, for this is the nearness of the ideal of truth to the realm of action. Men cannot act in general; they have to act specifically. So the options of action are narrowed—either this or that, or, at the most, that other—as in the field of truth it is tempting to say that it is either so or not so. But among the "not so's," the generous must find room for beauty and amplitude for goodness.

What is false to a linear logic may equally

well be described as good or beautiful from the vantage of a logic that is organic enough to plurality to allow for the whole of value. The recognition of such leeway is the first condition of its utilization. In the presence of the problematic, and so of the dubious, with which we all start, there would appear to be only this option: either we act coercively in the name of a narrow clarity, with terrors of a nuclear civilization added to facilitate universal suicide, or we graduate from the ideal of a compulsative clarity into such charity as admits the legitimacy, and joys in the fecundity, of plural meanings throughout the most sacred realm of the ideal.

With the latter alternative beckoning our better part, we are now prepared, as we were not in the previous chapter, to venture a definition of democracy, a triune definition generous enough to include and to reconcile both compromise and containment.

(1) As an ideology, democracy is such emphasis upon equality as stays liberty short of license and fraternity short of fanaticism; (2) as a way of life, democracy is ability to stomach, if not to love, variety; and (3) as a form of government, democracy is capacity to cooperate despite deep differences as to what is just and right.

Democracy is, in short, man's contemporary prompting to growth of soul, to spiritual heroism.

IV. *Two Kinds of Heroism*

Let us end our discussion, grown now progressively more abstract, with a return toward the concrete. In doing so we here but broach a subject which we have treated more fully elsewhere. It is clear that the eventuation of our present argument is in a certain type of character. Only the self-contained can practice creative compromise. Democracy makes high exactions of men, inwardly and outwardly. One modern democratic critic, George Santayana, has put the matter thus: "If a noble and civilized democracy is to subsist, the common citizen must be something of a saint and something of a hero." But there are two kinds of saints, as we have discerned: the dogmatic and the dynamic. There are also two kinds of heroes, as we are now to emphasize: the hero of commission and the hero of omission. There is Odysseus, justly renowned for what he did; there is Penelope, deserving of equal renown for what she did not do. Each of us is a child of both classic parents; we are all partly masculine but also partly feminine.

Our hero of commission is the doer of deeds. He is also, of course, the man of ideals. It is natural for men to have and to act upon ideals, for ideals are but generalized purposes, made the more urgent oftentimes because of vast postponement. To have an ideal is to be already launched toward action. We may say plainly indeed that heroism by commission is the accolade of successful action. It is celebrated in practical men who resolutely ride a purpose over great difficulties to the goal. It is found also in intrepid thinkers who hover "on the brink of the bottomless pit of reflection," undaunted by finding behind every cause another cause and back of every reason another reason. Our world is full of challenges, practical and intellectual, to this heroism of commission, rich in opportunities for distinction, and far from barren in resolute fulfillment of ideal purposes. But this heroism of active effort is not enough for the hour of authentic honor. Action is indispensable but insufficient. Each human agent must take as well as give.

This heroism of commission (lest heroes be vanquished by heroes) is made safe for the world by men, and especially by women, of strategic omission. Civilization more and more requires men who can stand and take it, as women have always done. Otherwise there is no resolution of equally stalwart but conflicting purposes short of somebody's getting liquidated in the name of an adamant ideal. Compromise is possible only between men who are severally informed of the grace of self-containment. This new type is able to stand and do his duty when the hour is stern; but he is also able not to make it his duty to do anything collectively until he can through

argument and persuasion and patience get at
least a majority of his fellows to agree upon the
wisdom or the necessity of proposed action.

Since there are a limited number of items on
the agenda of history which can beget and sustain majority agreement (and since even these
are tainted with compromise), this gentler type
of hero will be engaged more in keeping his ur-
gencies of infliction to himself than in implement-
ing his social ideals through the crucible of action.
To contemplate rather than to perpetrate will become an ideal of individual conduct; and, as
touching the collective, such a hero can compromise an issue without compromising himself, for
the simple reason that a very large sector of himself is withdrawn from action altogether, and so
made immune to its fevers. Such an one has
meat to eat which the do-gooder knows not of.
His is, in short, more a heroism of passion than of
action. This hero must be a politician, but one
who would minimize rather than maximize the
area of the political. What he contains as immune from compromise transcends what he compromises, both quantitatively and qualitatively.

The well known sacerdotal saints will not fully
meet our prescription—not Jesus nor Gandhi.
Socrates from ancient days approaches the ideal,
but at a distance. Abraham Lincoln is perhaps
our closest approximation in historic time to this
eidolon of character. How shall we describe the

type, which is easier to identify than to characterize? Lowes Dickinson, in commenting upon "Cambridge men," approaches what we have in mind:

It is a type, unworldly without being saintly, unambitious without being inactive, warm-hearted without being sentimental. Through good report and ill such men work on, following the light of truth as they see it; content to know what is knowable and to reserve judgment on what is not. The world could never be driven by such men, for the springs of action lie deep in ignorance and madness.

Aye, there's the rub: the heroism of this type is not in any sense trigger-happy. It will keep to the minimum the area of life rendered mediocre through compromise. We have already spoken of Lincoln's declaration that even with all power he would not have known what to do about slavery. This was, as he indicated, because of ambiguity so radical as to divide good men from men equally good. *"They* are," to repeat his crucial conclusion about the Southerners, "just what *we* would be in their situation." He who, in that manner, houses somehow in himself the dark conflicts of creed and the harsh incidence of clashing interests, emerges, if he manages to emerge at all, himself a brighter and a sweeter soul. What such an one deals with is always "too vast for malice." Emily Dickinson also says:

> And life is not so ample I
> Could finish enmity.

Something happens both positively and negatively to one who, like Lincoln, allows his own soul to become the battleground of the world of powers. The negative precipitate of such achievement is clear: our hero gets over the fever of fanaticism by becoming voluntary host in thought to opposites of action. Such a man develops magnanimity toward opponents because he sees that they but play, from their (dis)advantage, the role he plays from his vantage. This hero of omission can kill an enemy, but he cannot kick his corpse.

This metamorphosis, which can happen to human character because of an honest internalization of conflict, runs deep in every man who learns to contain his ideal impetuosities. He loses his innocence, to be sure—but when was innocence a moral virtue?—and he takes on a sense of strategy which is uncorrupted by any admixture of guile. Humility, a vice, is in him transformed into modesty, always a virtue; and impulses toward cynicism level out as pervasive sympathy. It is in this mystery of grace called containment that we find our truest recipe of democratic virtue.

The only visible chance to rise above power in nature and above compromise in politics is to internalize the natural and social struggle and let the alchemy of osmosis supplant the brute fact of power displacement. This is in imagina-

tion to sublimate the power struggle, dramati-
cally rehearsing the options of action available
until the desirable in idea unites with the desired
in fact. Such resolution of conflict achieves what
closely resembles a monism of plural values. The
good man may be, as has been said, one who
struggles successfully against himself, but the
great man is one who has come to terms with
himself through advance assimilation within him
of his own warring options. Human greatness is
the harmonious functioning of man's total powers, each unafraid of the other.

Our moral hero is he who in every situation
finds the grace to do what he can do without
foredooming himself to suffer fruitlessly from
what he cannot do. A man's strength is measured not by what he puts out, but by what he
saves back, by his reserves, and by the friction-
lessness of his functioning. Spiritual greatness
comes not by abnegation but by way of endur-
ance: of the inner tensions produced by the conflicts of the outer. The boundary of such a soul
is "a beyond that is within." No, it is not a doctrine of renunciation which we proclaim.

It is not the part of a man to foreswear the
heroism of action, for even the spiritual life rests
on animal foundations and involves commitment.
Heroism by commission is earned fruitage of par-
ticipation in the course of events. But the impetus to act gets adequate natural enforcement.

Instinct impels out-giving and ideals reinforce what instinct activates. What needs compensating aid is the impulse not to act—not to act audaciously or inconsiderately. Conscious and considerate control of action is indeed what forever requires and rewards cultivation.

Without the heroism of omission, the thinking of even great thoughts will undo the best of us. "To think great thoughts," says Justice Oliver Wendell Holmes, "you must be a hero as well as an idealist." The humblest ideal requires more of us than we can ever fulfil in action. So to escape paralyzing guilt, we must learn how to contain the surplus of action resident in every ideal. The tragic element in our individual vocation, and especially in our national vocation, goes further than wistfulness; it reaches deeper than tears.

It arises from the fact of conflict between ideals, but it does not stop short of this surplus of value inherent in every ideal. As to the conflicts, it is enough to repeat that not all good men have ever been agreed upon all goodness, not all just men on all justice, nor all holy men on all holiness. As to the doctrine of surplusage, it is sufficient for each man to resurrect from his own chastening experience the memory that no ideal is so humble as not to require of the idealist more than he can perform. It is as necessary, then, that the surplus of the ideal be contained as that the functional fringe of it be discharged. Not to contain the residue is to become in truth the tragic victim of all that is best in human life. Sara Teasdale learned the hard way that "compromises wait/ behind each hardly opened gate," and she wrote this her saddest poem, as prelude to suicide, a paean of dispraise to "the faultiness of things."

Men and women who escape suicide and who neither "get" nor "give" ulcers under the tensions of life and through the queasiness of cold war are those who have found their peace—and where else find it?—at the heart of the storm. "Positive thinking" has the power of benevolence only to those who can sustain the grace of negated action. The art of self-containment makes compromise honorable as touching outer things and unnecessary as touching the inner. It provides men substances to live on, ideals to live for, and semblances to live by.

Logical presumption, with which we began, gives way in the end to cosmic piety under the aegis of containment, and the heroes that emerge from its discipline can support not only themselves but each, besides, a few weakly leaning brothers. The super-moral is contained in Emerson's wise words: "It is easy in the world to live after the world's opinions; it is easy in solitude to live after our own; but the great man is he who in the midst of the crowd, keeps with perfect sweetness the independence of solitude."

Such souls are at once the heroic requirements and the heroic embodiments of civilization. As citizens, such characters can in very truth "compromise issues without compromising themselves." They can find, through ambiguity, a doorway to spiritual amplitude.

Index